A Girl's Guide to Understanding BOYS

Dannah Gresh & Suzy Weibel

HARVEST HOUSE PUBLISHERS
EUGENE, OREGON

Unless otherwise indicated, all Scripture quotations are from the Holy Bible, New Living Translation, copyright © 1996, 2004, 2007 by Tyndale House Foundation. Used by permission of Tyndale House Publishers, Inc., Carol Stream, Illinois 60188. All rights reserved.

Verses marked MSG are taken from The Message. Copyright © by Eugene H. Peterson 1993, 1994, 1995, 1996, 2000, 2001, 2002. Used by permission of NavPress Publishing Group.

Cover and interior design by www.DesignbyJulia.com, Woodland Park, Colorado

Cover photos © Jaimie Duplass / Shutterstock; Photodisc / Jupiterimages

Interior photos (numbers indicate page location):
  © Shutterstock, photographers as follows: 6-7 boy and girl: J.M. Gelpi; 7 girl: Raisa Kanareva; 9 boy: Mandy GodBeHear; 9 girl: Jack Hollingsworth; 10: Irina Tischenko; 15: Jaimie Duplass; 17: Samuel Borges; 19: R. Gino Santa Maria; 29: Creatista; 31: Jacek Chabraszewsk; 32: Werner Heiber; 37: rnl; 43: Tom Wang; 49: Andresr; 52: Michael Jung; 56: Jack Hollingsworth
  © Getty Images: 46, 90
  © Monkey Business Images: 24
  © Dan Seifert, Stone House Photography: 36, 38
  Steve Tressler, Mountainview Studios: 16, 44

Illustrations by Andy Mylin: 23, 52-53, 68, 69

Interior spot illustration and doodle graphics: Julia Ryan and Shutterstock.com

SECRET KEEPER GIRL is a registered trademark of Dannah Gresh.

A GIRL'S GUIDE TO UNDERSTANDING BOYS
Secret Keeper Girl® Series
Copyright © 2014 by Dannah Gresh
Published by Harvest House Publishers
Eugene, Oregon 97402
www.harvesthousepublishers.com

Library of Congress Cataloging-in-Publication Data
  Gresh, Dannah.
  A girl's guide to understanding boys / Dannah Gresh and Suzy Weibel.
      pages cm. — (Secret keeper girl series)
  ISBN 978-0-7369-5536-2 (pbk.)
  ISBN 978-0-7369-5537-9 (eBook)
  1. Man-woman relationships—Religious aspects—Christianity—Juvenile literature. 2. Boys—Psychology—Juvenile literature. 3. Girls—Religious life—Juvenile literature. I. Weibel, Suzy. II. Title.
  BT705.8.G74 2014
  248.8'2—dc23
                                                              2013015778

Printed in the United States of America

16 17 18 19 20 21 22 / VP-DBJ / 10 9 8 7 6 5 4 3 2

To all of our
Secret Keeper Girl fans.
We love meeting you
when we get the chance.

Boys are not gross. They are great! In fact, we especially like two of them and want to thank them for everything they do to make this book and the whole Secret Keeper Girl ministry work.

Bob and Jonathan, you are our best friends on the whole earth. We love that you like us. We like you, too. You sacrifice so much to let us write and travel to speak to our Secret Keeper Girls. Jonathan put it very well when he said, "People sometimes ask me if it is hard to be away from Suzy so she can travel to minister. I remind them how many little girls come to know Jesus through Secret Keeper Girl. This is our sacrifice for the kingdom." We love your kingdom hearts.

Thanks also to the boys...and girls...at Harvest House who make these books beautiful and "korect are spilling 'n gramr." The boys who worked hard on this project included Terry Glaspey and Paul Gossard. They wouldn't be a complete team without the girls: LaRae Weikert and Barb Sherrill.

Our friend Andy Mylin—who is also a boy—handcrafted the illustrations in this book. Julia Ryan, Secret Keeper Girl designer extraordinaire, designed the cover and internal pages. Isn't everything beautiful?

And thanks especially to Jesus, who has taught us how to interact with boys the way he intended. We hope you learn a lot about that in the pages of this book.

Dannah and Suzy

CONTENTS

A Note from
Dannah and Suzy

Boys. Yucky or not so bad? You may not think there's much need to talk about boys yet, but we think they are worth the time. After all, the Bible says that we have been created male and female to "reign over" this place called Earth together.

But boys are hard to understand, right? They don't think like us. They don't care about the things we do. They seem so…alien. Well, that's why we wrote this book. We both share a house with one of those alien creatures, and Dannah even has one for a son! Turns out they're not so bad after all. And we have some good insight for you on how to relate to them in all of their glorious boy-ness.

You've got this, Secret Keeper Girl!

God's Word gives us really clear guidelines about all areas of life. In its pages we find examples of people doing things God's way and succeeding…and choosing to do things their own way and failing miserably. We know one of the hardest parts about reading the Bible is making it work in the life you live today. So, we've created the Secret Keeper Girl Series. It's part modern-girl self-help and part Bible study so you can think through how God's truth can work in your real life.

Part one of this book—Everything You Need to Know About Boys—is self-help.

Self-help is the kind of book your parents read when they want to be a better parent or bookkeeper or gardener. In this case, you're reading it because you want to know how to relate to boys. Self-help books advise you on certain topics. You'll read a lot of them in your lifetime.

Don't worry if this is your first self-help book. You may be used to chapter books and fiction. So we've written it in that style and it'll be fun to read. You can do this part of the book alone.

Part two of this book—What God Says About Boys—is a Bible study.

A Bible study guides you through the Bible on a certain topic or book and enables you to do your own studying. You'll be reading Bible verses and answering questions about them, applying them to your life. There are even quizzes and games in this part. It's going to be fun. You'll have to put some work in to feel the thrill in your belly for this kind of fun! You can do the second part of the book alone, but it's much better if you do it with your mom or a group of girls.

FUN!

A Note from Dannah and Suzy

Part 1

Everything You Need to Know About Boys

Boys Are Gross, Right?

I, Suzy, grew up with two older brothers. In my house, everything was a competition. Dinnertime became an Olympic event called "Who Can Shove the Most Food into Their Mouth?" Crayons weren't for coloring. They were meant to be broken into little pieces and then thrown at passing cars through the back window of the station wagon. Whoever hit the most cars (or didn't get yelled at by Mom) won. And in a pool with boys, we couldn't just swim. Oh no. The pool had to involve contests of who could stay underwater the longest, who could swim the fastest, who could dunk whom, and who could do the best belly flop off the diving board.

One day I was the last to arrive at our backyard pool. My brothers and their friends were treading water and discussing various ways to jump from great heights into the deep end of the pool. Of course we all knew the pool rules: the only thing you jump off from is the diving board. But I had already jumped from the top of our slide, and I had seen one of my brothers' friends take a running start from the roof of the cabana and clear the concrete. Many possibilities remained to be explored.

At this point my brothers informed me they had been doing flips from the top of the slide. "Oh yeah," they said. "Didn't you see us from the house? We've all done one. But...you're probably too little. It's probably not something a girl can do."

Back then, there was a movie I'd seen called *Back to the Future*. The main character, Marty McFly, couldn't stand to be called a chicken. Call McFly a chicken and his eyes narrowed, his lip curled in a sneer, and he became defiantly brave. I had mastered the McFly lip curl for whenever I was told I probably couldn't do something because I was a girl.

"I can too," I told them, looking up uncertainly at the ten-foot-tall structure.

"Okay, I dare you," my brother Rick said. Our pool was not a rectangle. It was kidney-shaped, kind of like an amoeba. There was a good deal of concrete between the top of the slide and the deep end of the pool. I knew Mom and Dad's rule about not jumping off the slide was a good one. But even stronger than my sense of rule-following was the desire to be as good as the boys. I headed up the ladder with great resolve.

Standing at the top of the slide, I could see the kitchen window where Mom often spent time preparing dinner or washing dishes. Was she looking out the window now? I really hoped she would come running out the back door of the house and order me off the slide immediately. I didn't even care if she made me come in for the day or grounded me. I just wanted to be saved. But she didn't come out, and the boys kept taunting me from the edges of the pool. Finally, I climbed to the outside of the slide's protective railing, fixed my eyes on the spot I wished to enter the pool, leapt, twisted, and...kerplunk! I made it! I splashed breathtakingly into the center of the deep end and emerged spitting a mouthful of water into my tormentors' faces.

They didn't congratulate me or applaud. They didn't pat me on the back or welcome me into their club. Instead they looked at one another wide-eyed and exclaimed, "Sweet! It *can* be done!!" They had used me as their test dummy! I would either succeed, telling

11

them they could now try a flip too, or…splat! Here's the scary thing though. I wasn't mad at them. I was first shocked, and then proud. I had paved the way in a competition with my older brothers. I was the first one to complete a dangerous mission. (Yes, I was found out and grounded, but that's a story for another day.)

I looked up to my brothers. They seemed so strong and brave. And mean.

Lessons About Boys

It seems from the time I arrived on the scene as the baby of the family I was the target of all my brothers' "pranks," if that's what you can call them. My mom recalls watching my three-year-old brother stick out his chubby little leg to trip me as I learned to walk. When I was four, my then-seven-year-old brother delighted in sitting on my stomach and popping balloons in my face. By the time we were seven and ten, he would pinch me when Mom wasn't looking and I would punch him in return. I was almost always seen, and he would cackle with delight as I received the scolding. Mean, right?

But most of the time I was not the punching bag. Most of the time my brothers, three and six years older than me, were my greatest cheerleaders and defenders. They included me in sports. We rode bikes together, swam for hours on end, practiced climbing trees and walking on log fences. We skied in Colorado and scuba dived in the Cayman Islands, and I watched dejectedly as they left for their guys-only fishing trip in Tennessee each summer. My brothers were my best buddies growing up, and in many ways I learned all of my early lessons about what a boy is from these two guys.

Are boys smelly? Yes! Take it from me! To this day I can smell the grass and sweat from their football uniforms as they dumped everything to be washed in the laundry room.

are boys smelly? yes!

They burped a lot, as well as being delighted with other body noises both real and faked.

But are boys gross? No. Psalm 139:14 says, "Thank you for making me so wonderfully complex! Your workmanship is marvelous—how well I know it." That verse isn't only about girls. In fact, a guy—King David—wrote those words. Just like you and I have been fearfully and wonderfully made, so have those boys we are talking about. Yes, those smelly, loud creatures who laugh at things that aren't even funny and are just plain awkward when life gets serious...they are fearfully and wonderfully made!

The first guy, Adam, was made from dirt!

You know, it's interesting to think back to the time of creation. The first guy (Adam) was made from the dirt. Seems appropriate. Maybe that's the reason guys are so comfortable with grass stains and mud. It's what they were born from! The first girl (Eve) was formed in a much different way. God caused Adam to fall into a deep sleep and he removed one of Adam's ribs. From this genetic material he formed the first woman.

> "The LORD God caused the man to fall into a deep sleep. While the man slept, the LORD God took out one of the man's ribs and closed up the opening. Then the LORD God made a woman from the rib, and he brought her to the man" (Genesis 2:21-22).

God could have made you and me from the dust of the ground. He proved it by creating Adam. But he chose to make females "out of" man. This way we know God's intentions for sure. We are not two separate species battling it out for who is the best or the strongest or God's favorite. We are one.

God knits each of us together as we grow in Mom's womb, some male and some female, but we all come from the same

13

original human being. Just like you have been given a unique personality, so has every boy you know. Do you worry about your future sometimes? Do you sometimes get mad at yourself for being a little lazy, saying the wrong things, or messing everything up… again? So does every boy you know.

Of Course, There Are Differences

1 Our conversations are different. Girls tend to enjoy talking about personal things, especially about friendships. Boys tend to talk more about sports and technology. I, Dannah, don't really like football. (Suzy likes it enough for both of us.) But my husband knows that if he will tell me the stories of the players on the field, I'll be engrossed. So he tells me who just got engaged, or how a certain player grew up without a dad. This brings our conversation together. Bob knows our conversations are different and so he blends them together! (Smart man.)

2 Our brains are different. Boys are typically only good at thinking about one thing at a time. When they solve problems, they like to do so in orderly steps. This usually gives them an amazing ability to focus. Have you ever seen your brother or your dad concentrating on a problem, a game, or fixing something—and not even hear or see what's happening around them? That's because they're able to put all their energy into one single task or activity.

Girls, however, have a "bridge" between the right (creative) and left (logical) sides of the brain that boys simply do not have. Thus we can think about more than one problem at a

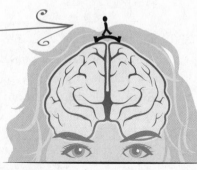

time and are able to go back and forth between several activities while problem-solving. You may be talking over the day's events with a girlfriend while folding clothes for your mom and helping your little brother with his math. This is sometimes called "multitasking." Have mercy on the guys...they're usually not very good at it!

3 **Our emotions are different.** Though boys experience every emotion we girls do, they are better at setting emotions aside while they work together. This is why a boy who is your friend one minute may seem to be totally ignoring you in science lab the next, or why a boy can tell his lab partner to "back off and let me do it," and then you may see the two laughing hysterically one minute later. What do feelings have to do with problem solving? That's how boys think. Not we girls! Relationship is everything, and life is something to be experienced and figured out together! Nothing is more devastating for a girl than to be "left out."

back off and let me do it

Yep, boys and girls are so different that sometimes we may as well be two different species! Of course, not all girls are emotional and not all boys are bad at multitasking. These are generalizations. That is to say, most of the time girls and boys are a certain way, but not all the time. That's okay too—but why did God make

THINK ABOUT IT

It's not just human boys who enjoy running straight at one another and crashing. The behavior is common with male goats, oxen, elk, sheep—and once upon a time with a little dinosaur about the size of a large dog, called the Stegoceras - validum. Its skull actually had an extra layer of protection to prevent brain damage from frequent head-butting. Know any boys who could use that extra layer?

us different enough that we sometimes get competitive? (Ever hear someone shout, "Girls rule—Boys drool"?)

Let's be careful. We weren't meant to live boys vs. girls. We were created different so that we could complement one another. God made us the perfect fit to

boys aren't so gross after all

"fill the earth and govern it. Reign over the fish in the sea, the birds in the sky, and all the animals that scurry along the ground" (Genesis 1:28). God told Adam and Eve to take care of his world *together*.

When we're older? As married couples one day? Sure. But even now! As classmates. As brother and sister. As kids. As teammates. God has created two of a kind, different but very similar, and we work together perfectly.

Really
THINK ABOUT IT!

Go to Meditation #1 in Part 2. The title is "What Does God Say About Boys?"

One of the best things you can do on this journey to understanding boys is to simply let them be boys. If we as girls can stop expecting boys to think like we do, talk like we do, reason like we do, and behave like we do, then we are way ahead of the game! Boys aren't so gross after all. They are just different. And this turns out to be part of God's plan. We were made to thrive in a world filled with variety!

aren't so gross after all

BOYS

2

Liking Boys Is Normal... What's Wrong with Normal?

It's "normal" for cats to be curious, but have you ever heard the saying "Curiosity killed the cat"? This phrase means when we are consumed by our interest or curiosity in something, we could be in danger. No one knows this better than a cat owner. Curiosity has led my (Suzy's) cat, Gray-Vee, into a dryer (we found her just before we turned it on), behind the kitchen cabinets where she was briefly stuck and was only freed because my daughter Marie has really bendy elbows, and 60 feet up a tree. The tree situation was a big problem... Gray-Vee couldn't figure out how to get back down.

At first we tried to ignore her. She meowed all through dinner, as we tried to play cards on the porch, while we got ready for bed, and all through the night. I must have opened my eyes every hour on the hour only to hear her pitiful howl. The next morning, worried she was going without food and water, we tried to take matters into our own hands.

Since cats are supposed to be able to survive a fall from a tree, we decided to help Gray-Vee along. We grabbed several tennis rackets and a bucket of old tennis balls and began lobbing shots in her direction. We were hoping to scare her off balance, and it

THINK ABOUT IT

Cats suffer fewer injuries from falling 50 feet or more than they do from falling short distances. A falling cat approaches the ground more like a parachute than like an airplane.

wasn't out of the question to literally knock her off a branch with a well-placed shot. Not one shot connected, and she looked confused as to why we were launching objects at her.

Next we brought out the 40-foot ladder. I was elected to be the climber. Though Gray-Vee came to me on the ladder, she would not let me grab her with my hands. Instead, she panicked and climbed back up to 60 feet.

My daughter went online and researched cat rescue methods. "Hey!" she emerged from the house waving her arms. "This article claims that if we put something up there she associates with safety, like her bed or her litter box, she'll jump into it."

My husband, Jonathan, was in charge of duct-taping the litter box to a long pole. Just before I climbed the 40-foot ladder a second time, I warned him, "She may jump or even fall. If she does, try to catch her. Do not let her hit the ground if you can help it." I doubted the truth of the "cats can survive a big fall" legend. (Nor did I know this would go down in history as the event that proved my hubby is not a professional duct-taper.) Sure enough, the cat made a beeline for her litter box. She climbed in without any hesitation.

I could tell immediately it would be tough to balance her weight on that little pole, but I didn't have much time to contemplate balance. The duct tape on the pole immediately gave way, catapulting Gray-Vee's little four-pound body into the air. She immediately proved her worth as an acrobat. Her head whipped around to the front, she positioned her legs underneath her and arched her back, giving her the appearance of a little gray-and-white parachute dropping from heaven. Jonathan was right underneath her and all he could think was, *This is soooo beautiful. It's magical!*

Until he managed to think, *Oh stink—she has claws.*

At the last second, when the cat was two inches from his outstretched hands, he stepped back and dropped his hands, not wanting to be clawed by a freaked-out cat. Gray-Vee hit a pile of leaves under the tree with a soft thud, where our Golden Retriever, Biscuit, immediately pounced upon her. (Yes, our pets are named Biscuit and Gray-Vee, but that's not the point.)

Lesson learned: it is natural for cats to climb trees. Climbing down is not as natural.

Sure, It's "Normal," But...

You have probably noticed that it's "normal" for your friends to talk about boys. The older you get, the more you will hear them talk. And this world will indeed tell you this is normal. And it probably is. I can remember (from as young as five years old) the first question my aunts and uncles would ask when I went to family parties: "So do you have a boyfriend?" Now, my aunts and uncles didn't seriously think a five-year-old girl would have a boyfriend, but they knew it was a funny question. And they were conditioning me. They were telling me what was expected. Girls are supposed to have boyfriends.

I took the advice to heart

I took the advice to heart. In my seventh-grade year I kept a diary where I recorded all of my daily thoughts. Most were about boys I liked or boys I hoped would notice me. Why did all of my friends have boyfriends? Why did they get to skate during the couples-only skating rounds at the roller rink while I had to watch from the sidelines?

These are all normal thoughts, but here is where life gets interesting. What if instead of chasing after what is normal, we choose to be girls who let God have the first and last word in everything we say and do? We would end up looking a little crazy for sure, but that's kind of how he wants us to be. Check this verse out:

"If I acted crazy, I did it for God…Christ's love has moved me to such extremes. His love has the first and last word in everything we do" (2 Corinthians 5:13-14 MSG).

We aren't supposed to be normal. Or boy-crazy. We're supposed to be God-crazy, and that means God gets to decide how we live. Not the world. In fact, the Bible says this:

"Don't copy the behavior and customs of this world, but let God transform you into a new person by changing the way you think. Then you will learn to know God's will for you, which is good and pleasing and perfect" (Romans 12:2).

We already know there is a difference between us and what the Bible calls "the world." So what is this "world" the Bible talks about, and are we a part of it or not?

We are definitely *in* the world. Just take a look around you at everything God has created. I have been so fortunate to grow up in a traveling family. I have seen pyramids in both Egypt and Mexico. I've leaned over the edge of the Grand Canyon and have swum in the bluer-than-blue waters of the Cayman Islands. I've seen the lake districts of both New York and Germany. When God looked around at his creation in the beginning, he saw that it was *good*! God's world is *GOOD*! And he loves the world. In fact, I can pretty much guarantee the stars still delight his eyes and that he loves watching dolphins playing in the waves every bit as much as you and I do. Puppies and kittens probably make him laugh. Why do I think this? I'm his kid and I'm just like him…and puppies and kittens delight me.

He also loves the *people* of this world. I'll bet you can fill in these blanks:

God loved the _____ so much that he gave his one and only

_____ , so that everyone who _____ in him will not

_____ but have eternal _____ (John 3:16).

Even though God loves this world and its people, we are not *of* this world. Not if we belong to God. The world, as great as it is, has been seriously scarred by sin. It's a broken world (that's why there are things like earthquakes and hurricanes), and our lives are here only for a short time. This world is not our home. We are the King's kids, and that makes us citizens of heaven. What this means is that we have to live under the rules of heaven, not this world's understanding of normal.

What If You Settle for Normal?

It may be normal by this world's standards to chase boy after boy after boy. It may be normal for aunts and uncles to tease you about little boyfriends. It may be normal for you to suddenly wake up one day and think, *"Hey, boys aren't so gross after all!"* But the thing is, God doesn't want us to be normal. He wants us to be crazy!

Here are some things happening to girls who settle for normal. We'll use my life as an example because I was a pretty "normal" girl, and I didn't know until I was a little older what it meant to be a citizen of heaven.

God wants us to be crazy!

1 **Hearts get broken.** For a long time I was desperate to be noticed. I figured the only way I could know for sure that I was pretty was if there was a boy who liked me. I didn't care who the boy was. *Anyone* would do. How do I know this for a fact? I said so in my diary. *"I'm desperate for someone, anyone, to notice me."* I spent a lot of days in the dumps when I should have been enjoying my friendship with girls and the affirmation of my family.

2 **Fights break out.** Have you noticed your girlfriends fighting a lot? It's normal...but completely unbecoming of a girl. I was

so jealous of my friends who had boyfriends. It meant they were better than me, right? Of course not, but that was the lie I told myself. I don't know about you, but when I feel threatened another feeling arises—the need to defend myself. If I had decided to be content with what I had (like a family that traveled a lot, good friends, and the ability to excel in sports and school) I would not have been so jealous of girls who had what I thought I wanted—boys.

3 Normal becomes…well…REALLY normal and overrides "crazy." What in the world does that mean? The longer I spent chasing one thing (being noticed and approved), the more it felt like "home." When I wasn't around the drama of another broken heart or yet one more fight with a girlfriend, life felt…well, boring. At some point normal (drama) becomes the *only* normal. But we were meant for something better! You are a masterpiece created by God. You are special. Don't you want to act like it?

What You Feed Grows

It all comes down to what we choose to "feed." We can feed our desire to be like *the world*—taking our cues from the *normal* boy-crazy girls at school or from stories about dating we watch on Nick at Nite. Or we can feed our desire to be a special part of *God's kingdom* in our hearts—taking our cues from the Bible, our parents, and other older, godly people. And that might mean we look a little crazy, but that's OK!

Here's a story that might tell you how important feeding the right one can be. A man once brought home two baby iguanas. He named one Liberty and the other Justice. Clever, huh? Liberty and Justice had everything in common. They lived in the same 55-gallon tank, with one heat lamp keeping both of them comfortable. They had plenty of water to drink and an awesome rock to "sun"-bathe on. There was only one thing these two iguanas did differently. Liberty ate huge amounts of fruit, veggies, and crickets. As a result he grew up big and strong. Justice, on the other hand, was a picky eater. He grew paler and paler in color, could not stand up to Liberty in a fight, and eventually gave up altogether. Liberty was left alone to rule the aquarium.

crazy...eat fruits and veggies and you rule!

We have a choice of which appetite to feed—the one to be normal and follow the "world's" ways, or the one to be special and to follow God's plan. The appetite we feed will grow bigger and will rule our lives.

Check out Romans 12:2 again: "Don't copy the behavior and customs of this world, but let God transform you into a new person by changing the way you think. Then you will learn to know God's will for you, which is good and pleasing and perfect."

Considering all of this, do you really want to be normal? Who's ready to be changed, grow up, and maybe do things in a way that's a little different? I hope you are!

Really
THINK ABOUT IT!

Go to Meditation #2 in Part 2. It's called "What Does God Say About Being Boy-Crazy?"

3

What Is Dating?

I guess my mom spotted it long before I (Suzy) did…that I wasn't ready for dating. One of my earliest "dating" experiences was with a boy named Tim. (There are so many Tims out there I won't even change the name to protect the innocent.) Tim really, really, really, really liked me, and as far as I can tell this was the first time such a thing had occurred in my life. He actually *liked* me, even when we were doing things like playing golf or eating dinner at the mall with my mom. He liked spending time with *me*.

I liked him too, in the sense that we had fun together. I thought he was cute. It seemed kind of cool to say, "Yeah, I'm dating someone." Today you might say, "I'm talking with someone" or "going out together" or "being together." Whatever you call it, what *is* it? I had no idea, and I definitely wasn't ready for it.

One of my earliest clues I wasn't ready was that I never wanted to talk to Tim on the phone. He would call every night like clockwork. I dislike telephones to this day so I was never in a rush to pick it up. Typically I was downstairs reading a book or watching a mindless TV show—either way, an interruption from the telephone was the last thing I wanted. Didn't matter who was on the other end, but it was *Tim*.

My mom, who was gently trying to help me see that I wasn't ready for this relationship, was always taking note of the conversations and followed up on them each day. "Didn't Tim just call you?" she would ask. And I would shrug. "Eh. I just spent all day with him at school. What in the world would we still have to talk about?" What I was telling her in so many words was that I, her little girl, wanted to remain a little girl for a little while longer.

And that I wasn't ready for dating.

THINK ABOUT IT

What do you think dating is? Ask someone else. What do they say it is?

★★☆

Defining "Dating"

Sometimes it's fun to go to a formal source for the definition of a word. For example, the dictionary says "school" is "an institution designed for the teaching of students (or 'pupils') under the direction of teachers." It sounds so formal that way, doesn't it?

The definition for "dating" is equally formal:

> "A form of courtship consisting of social activities done by two people with the aim of each assessing the other's suitability as a partner in an intimate relationship or as a spouse. While the term has several meanings, it usually refers to the act of meeting and engaging in some mutually agreed upon social activity in public, together, as a couple" (Wikipedia).

Whew, that's a mouthful! Let's break it down and put it in conversational language, because it's not a bad definition for our foundation. We'll mix in the cement of God's truth as we go along. This won't be an easy task...dating isn't even mentioned in the Bible!

Dating is a form of courtship.

Dating is, as we often say to kids in our church, a school for marriage. *Courtship* is an old word dating back to the time when nearly every country had a king and queen. When people wanted something from the king he would "hold court." This means people could come into his presence and ask for whatever favors they might have. Likewise, a king might "hold court" for visitors from other countries whom he wanted to impress.

DATING DEFINITION #1

Dating should wait until you're beginning to feel ready for marriage.

Courtship plans to first impress someone and then ask for something. (As in, "Will you marry me?") When I "dated" Tim, there was no chance of marriage anytime soon and we both knew it. Until you're old enough to consider marriage, dating leads only to frustration!

DATING DEFINITION #2

Dating is a verb, not a state of being. It means actually *going* somewhere and *doing* something. Until Mom and Dad let us off the leash, it's not even really possible to date.

Dating is a social event.

Dating is active. It's social. The first time I ever "dated" someone was in middle school. I could not drive, my parents did not approve, and I still had a bedtime. The only chance I had to see this boy was during school. School is social to a degree, but I wouldn't exactly call math class a date. I didn't brag to the girls about the nice meal he took me out for...at the school cafeteria. We didn't date or go out. We did what we called "going together," and all it really meant was that each of us got to say someone liked us.

Dating is exclusive.

A dating relationship, just like marriage, is meant to be exclusive. That means you won't be shared with anyone else. And you have no plan to look at or talk with another guy. It's for just one guy and one girl. That means a date (going out to do something social for one evening) is different than dating or being together. Back in my middle-school "going together" experience, my heart and mind were not exclusive. One day I wrote in my diary, "I like Jason!" The very next day I wrote, "I'm going with Doug!" Poor Doug! I liked Jason…didn't I? One week later I was mad at Doug for not going to a skating party, so I skated with a bunch of other guys. That showed him!

Did it, though? Did I show Doug? Or was I teaching myself to step up to a smorgasbord and select as many items as I wanted? Boys aren't "items." Each one is God's masterpiece just like you and me. Each one has feelings and hopes and dreams and insecurities. None of that mattered to me because I wasn't ready to date.

DATING DEFINITION #3

In dating, relationship is defined by two people who like only each other, just like marriage. Never date just so you can say someone likes you.

Dating is a job interview.

Dating is a chance to find out if a boy could possibly fill the job of husband. There are a lot of nice guys out there, but "nice" is not always "right." One of my (Suzy's) husband's favorite things to do is show off my glove. (Sounds weird, right?) I was the first girl in my town to play Little League baseball. When I made the team I had short hair, the coaches couldn't see my name, and they totally thought they had picked a boy. This, frankly, really upset me!

Anyhow, to this very day I have maintained a good glove and a strong arm. So my husband will take a baseball and bring it at me as hard as he possibly can. He played college baseball and even had a pro-baseball tryout, so the ball hums pretty good when he throws it. It makes his mom furious. She's so afraid I'm going to get hurt. But she also has to admit and has said it many times, "God gave Jonathan the perfect wife. I don't think anyone could handle him but you." I don't think she's talking about handling his throws either. It's probably more along the lines of keeping him organized and being able to make him laugh. (We're still working on things like picking up his dirty socks.)

DATING DEFINITION #4

Dating should start with an informal interview to determine if this guy is the kind of guy you really can spend your whole life with!

When I was old enough to consider marriage, I "dated" a lot of guys who did not pass my "job" interview. But when I was younger there was no interview. Instead it went something like this: *You like me? Really? Awesome! I guess I'll like you too.* It didn't matter what we had in common or how much we agreed on things—I wanted to date any boy that I could. I regret that. It was silly. I have a lot of respect for young girls who don't do what I did.

Some girls take time during their teen years to think and pray about what they want in a husband. I (Dannah) did this. (But not until I realized, like Suzy, that I wasn't ready to date!) While I was waiting for the right time, I wrote a list of qualities I was looking for in a husband. In addition to some silly things like "having great eyes," my list included "totally going after God" and also required him to have some of the same interests and passions that I have, including animals. (Today we have a farm with llamas, horses, goats, peacocks, and more!) Woulda been a bummer to end up with a guy who didn't love them like I do!

Don't Start Dating Until You're Ready, Because Dating Is Dangerous

We have come to the conclusion that we had no business dating before college. That is our opinion, but you should have your own opinion too. Let your parents help you decide when you're ready. Sometimes parents say their daughters can date earlier than college, but you really need to let them decide this. Not your friends or the "normal" world!

Now that we know a little more of what dating actually is, we hope it will help you rethink how you spend the rest of your tween years! You are not ready to date. (We hope that doesn't hurt your feelings. It's just because we care that we tell you this at all.) Is dating bad,

is dating bad, then?

then? No. Dating isn't bad. It's just dangerous. And *dangerous* and *bad* are not the same thing. Think about it. Scuba diving... love it! Dangerous! Skydiving...looks fun! Dangerous! Being at the top of a cheerleading pyramid, getting flipped in the air, doing two somersaults, and landing in the arms of three other cheerleaders... whee! Dangerous!

And why is dating dangerous? Here are just a couple of reasons, though there may be more.

1 **First of all,** *many (we're afraid most) girls who begin to date a boy become consumed by the relationship.* It's the only thing they can think about or talk about. We plead guilty! When we liked a boy and wanted to spend time with him, he got first priority in our lives. We would ditch our girlfriends to talk to him. We would lie about where we were going so our friends wouldn't be mad. Sadly, we did the same to God during these times. If the only thing on a girl's mind is a boy, she's not going to be spending time with God. The problem is, spending time with God is the only thing that prepares us for successful dating.

2 **Second,** dating is also dangerous simply for the fact that *dating has only one of two outcomes.* It either ends in marriage (which shouldn't be on your radar for years yet) or it just ends. Heartbreaks are no laughing matter. Breakups hurt even when true love isn't involved, because the message we receive still feels like, "You are not wanted" and "You are not beautiful." Of course, these things are not true. What's true is that you are in middle school and not ready for dating, but we girls have hearts that get very mixed up.

There is one thing that makes dating less dangerous: knowing the goal. It's not to have a boyfriend or to feel affirmed. It's not to fit in or to be popular. The goal of dating is *marriage*. Knowing that makes it less dangerous because you won't get caught up in the normalcy of dating too soon.

In the Bible, the apostle Paul wrote that all of life is like running a race. We run to win the prize. This means we have to look at the finish line. The finish line of dating is marriage. Dating too soon makes us look silly.

There is a hilarious YouTube video called Silly Olympics. It poses questions like, "What if there were a race for people with no sense of direction?" When the starting gun is fired, these athletes run off in

the finish line of dating is marriage

ten different directions. (Can you just imagine the 200-meter pool race for nonswimmers?) It is cry-out-loud funny. But maybe it's a good reminder for us of just how silly we look when we date too soon. One question posed in the video is, "What if we had a marathon for people with weak bladders?" The video shows people sprinting for about three steps and then desperately running off the road to relieve themselves in the woods. They never get anywhere because they have to "go."

You'll never get anywhere dating if you're not ready for it. Don't date until you're ready to run to the finish line.

Really
THINK ABOUT IT!

Go to Meditation #3 in Part 2. It's called "Who Does God Say Gets to Decide When I Start to Date?"

RUN!

4

How Should I Act Around Boys?

et's say your pastor has invited you to speak in front of the whole church. He wants you to tell the story of how your life was radically changed when you went on a missions trip with your family last summer. You're excited to talk about how you were really touched by how sweet the little kids in the village were. You noticed that they had very few possessions, and their dolls and stuffed animals all looked like they came from a war zone. But they were really happy. You determined to give away a lot of your toys and clothes when you came home, now that you were aware not every kid in the world had a closet as full as yours. You quit spending as much time at the mall when you came home and stopped bugging your mom to let you wear makeup. You were generally a happier girl—content with what you had.

As you get ready for your talk, it occurs to you that a certain cute boy is going to be there. I mean, you've never talked to him, and you're not really allowed to "date" or anything, but *he's* going to be there. Looking at *you*. Suddenly you're not thinking anymore about how your experience on the mission field might encourage someone else to be content or to care about the poor. You're just thinking about how to get noticed. You spend an hour on your nails. Mom has to scold you for being in the shower too long. You try on four different outfits. *Why don't I have any cute clothes? Oh, that's right. I gave them all away this summer. I need to go to the mall.*

It's time to leave for church and it hits you. You forgot to finish writing your talk! You forgot to put together a slide presentation of some of your photos like you promised.

This, my friend, is a fashion faux pas. (A "faux pas"—pronounced *foh pah* because it's French—is a terribly unacceptable social error!)

What Are You Wearing?

Let me explain. There are two kinds of fashion.

1 **External fashion.** The first kind is what we wear or pay attention to on the outside. We are not against external fashion at SKG (Secret Keeper Girl). It's fun to put together outfits that immediately say, "Hey, you've never met me before, but this is kind of who I am as a person!"
Our clothing and accessory choices do convey to others if we are artsy, fussy, casual, sporty, fun, or sometimes even if we're angry. That's kind of how it goes with clothes!

2 **Internal fashion.** But there's another kind of fashion world going on inside every one of us. Colossians 3 talks about all kinds of outfits we are supposed to dress up in on our insides.

We'll look at that more deeply in our Bible study for this chapter, but think about it. If your outside fashion says something about who you are, how much more does your inside fashion communicate to people?

We may want to believe no one can see what is in our heart, but in Matthew 12:34 the Bible says whatever is in our heart determines what we say. One version of the Bible says the mouth speaks what the heart is full of. Our behaviors and the words we speak, even the clothes we choose to wear to some degree, are indicators of what is in our hearts.

It's actually very easy to see what you are wearing inside…on your heart.

And one of the places where we can see what a girl is wearing on her heart is how she acts around boys. Frankly, a lot of girls are just wearing boy-crazy, attention-grabbing, self-serving stuff on the inside, and it shows up in the way they act and appear on the outside.

In fact, actions tell us much more about a person than outward appearances, which don't necessarily tell us the whole truth. Do you remember how God sent a prophet named Samuel to anoint a new king for Israel? Samuel knew he would choose from the sons of a man named Jesse, but he had no idea which son to anoint. When he saw the first and oldest son, tall and handsome, he was sure this young man was meant to be king. But God corrected Samuel.

> "The Lord said to Samuel, 'Don't judge by his appearance or height, for I have rejected him. The Lord doesn't see things the way you see them. People judge by outward appearance, but the Lord looks at the heart'" (1 Samuel 16:7).

The king God had in mind was of course David. David was the youngest of the brothers, and he was a simple shepherd boy. He wasn't even old enough to shave yet. He was so small that battle armor didn't fit him. You and I would never say, "That kid is fit to be a king!" But God did.

Are you boy-crazy or God-crazy?

We have a friend who was absolutely boy-crazy in middle school. We'll call her Kate. She screamed when her favorite pop artists began to sing. When she was allowed to go on her first trip with the youth group, she spent all her time taking pictures with boys and posting them on Facebook. At any given time, she had two or three boys on the line to go out with her. To us and most of her peers, she looked very silly. And internally, her heart was not wearing classy stuff.

But a friend of hers pulled her aside and told her, "Kate, you are boy-crazy and you're supposed to be God-crazy!" For a while, Kate was mad, but she heard her friend, and soon she made a decision to get control of her behavior. She eventually became one of the most beautifully dressed (think: *inside*) girls we have ever seen. She started really listening to what her youth pastor said and took notes in her journal. Instead of following every move Justin Bieber made, she got hooked on following every move that Jesus made.

So how do you act around boys? Do you put on clothes to impress? Do you giggle more than necessary? Do you act the same around Mom and Dad, your best friends, and the boys? Or do you put on an act?

How Should You Act Around Boys?

So the bottom line is this: How should you act around boys? Well, you probably shouldn't act like everyone else around you. This won't be easy! So here are a few tips:

1 **Don't be boy-crazy.** In Ephesians 4:17 the apostle Paul says, "I insist—and God backs me up on this—that there be no going along with the crowd, the empty-headed mindless crowd" (MSG).

When my (Dannah's) daughter Lexi was in middle school there was hardly a girl in her school that wasn't boy-crazy. Lexi felt really lonely, but she stayed off the boy-crazy train and eventually some of her friends joined her! You'll stick out in a crowd if you stay off the boy-crazy train. (Translation: you won't be normal, you'll be special.)

2 Do your work. We shouldn't lose sight of more important things like speaking notes and slides or homework or church. One of our internal garments is hard work! "Work hard so you can present yourself to God and receive his approval. Be a good worker" (2 Timothy 2:15).

3 Do treat guys like good friends, not potential dates. Hebrews 13:1 says, "Keep on loving each other as brothers and sisters." You and I are supposed to be full of love for guys...but not romantic love. Brotherly love. Would you worry about your biological brother seeing you sweat? No! So play hard when you play kickball. Stop fussing with your hair or painting your nails to impress. (It's okay if you like doing your hair and nails, but don't let a boy be your motivation.) Chill! Be cool. They are brothers, not boyfriends.

Really
THINK ABOUT IT!

Go to Meditation #4 in Part 2. It's called "How Does God Want Me to Act Around Boys?"

These actions are not things you can fake. The outside will always let others know what the inside looks like. Start with your heart. We're gonna have to go much deeper for this one so let's get to it in our Bible study!

So How Can I Help My Boy-Crazy Friends?

Is there any help for the boy-crazy girl? Do you know anyone who is boy-crazy? (Maybe it's you.)

I, Suzy, wasn't always boy-crazy. When I was a tween (that's technically between the ages of eight and twelve) I was all about sports. Baseball was my favorite. Not softball. See, I grew up in the dark ages when sports teams were not popular for girls. It wasn't quite the dark ages of my grandma, though. I have seen pictures of her middle-school basketball team. Their uniforms were *skirts*! Can you imagine playing basketball in a skirt? I don't think it probably looked like the game we play today!

But let's go back to baseball. My town had Little League baseball, but no softball teams for girls. That program just didn't exist yet. See? Dark ages. If I wanted to play ball, it was going to have to be baseball. By the time I tried out for Little League at age 11, girls had only been allowed to play Little League for two years, and I was the first girl ever to try out in Fort Wayne, Indiana.

I remember standing on the pitching mound with all the boys who were trying out for teams. We had each been given a number to wear, and this was the only way coaches could identify us. They didn't know our names, and as players we didn't know each other's names either. We were busy drawing our initials into the dirt with our toes while we waited our turn to pitch, guessing names as we went along.

I carefully toed an *S* into the dirt. "Steve!" One of the boys guessed. This took me by surprise. I wasn't in disguise or anything, but come to think of it I was sending out a few confusing signals. I was wearing a baseball hat. I had short hair. And to look at the front of my T-shirt…well, I didn't exactly have need for a bra yet, if you get what I'm saying. I was dressed like everyone else. Jeans. Tee. Hat. "Scott!" Another guess was shouted out. "I'm a girl," I announced. Crickets. They had no idea what to say so they just let the next guy start drawing his initials in the dirt while they kept a polite distance from me, the intruder.

For two years I was kind of one of the guys. I don't mean to say I wanted to be a boy. I totally didn't. I just wanted to play baseball. I wanted to be told I was good. I wanted to strike batters out. I wanted to hit home runs. It never occurred to me that the boys on my team were anything more than teammates.

I needed MY FRIENDS to step up and rescue me.

When the boy-crazy train hit me I was completely unprepared. One day I was fielding ground balls with my teammates and the next day, with no warning, the boy playing shortstop was the cutest thing I had ever seen. Yep, that's the same boy who had been just another teammate only yesterday.

Can Friends Really Help?

First let me explain there is a group of professional people out there called "behaviorists" whose job is to study human behavior and the normal workings of society. The work they do is called research, and it is considered a science. When they write and share their findings, they are saying, "Here's how human behavior and society work in most cases." These research professionals have found that the number-one influence in a young person's life is her family, especially her parents.

As you move toward your teens, your parents are still the most important people, but a lot of their work is done, and friends become increasingly more important. This is a little bit dangerous, and here's why. Other researchers, ones who study the makeup of the human body and brain, have found that the human brain does not fully develop until people are more than 20 years old! This means the best person to take direction from is not going to be a 12-year-old, even if that 12-year-old is currently your favorite person on the face of the planet.

I needed my friends, yes. But my friends still needed *their* parents.

I (Dannah) remember a time in sixth grade when I needed my parents to help me. I had a friend who we'll call Dorrie. She was as boy-crazy as they come. One weekend she and I went to our local church camp, Summit Grove, to help clean it up for the summer.

Despite all my pleading, my slightly older seventh-grade friend kept flirting with even older boys. My heart was pounding like a drum when she showed up to help a group of us paint a fence wearing nothing but *my* swimsuit. (She hadn't even asked.) The rest of us were in sweatpants and T-shirts, but there was nothing but some spandex between the guys in our group and her brand-new curves! (And Dorrie, unlike Suzy, *did* need a bra!) A youth leader made her put on some shorts and a T-shirt, but later she snuck off with one of the guys, and I saw her taking her T-shirt off as she went.

To be honest, I didn't know what to do. She wasn't listening, and something in me just knew Dorrie was in for a bad time if she didn't change her behavior toward guys. I was afraid.

When we got home, my mom was unpacking my suitcase and found my swimsuit. She wasn't too happy that it was covered in white paint. That's when it all poured out. I told my mom everything, and she got on the phone with Dorrie's mom in no time. They were like experts. The two of them knew just what to say to Dorrie and how to help her. I didn't.

Do you turn the big stuff over to the experts? The Bible has a lot to say about going to wise people for advice! Here are some gems just from Proverbs 13:

> "Those who take advice are wise" (verse 10).
> "People who despise advice are asking for trouble" (verse 13).
> "The instruction of the wise is like a life-giving fountain" (verse 14).
> "Walk with the wise and become wise" (verse 20).

Your friends need you, yes, but you need the wisdom of the experts in your life. Those experts may be Mom and Dad, they may be Grandma and Grandpa, or they may even be the parents of a good friend or a youth leader.

You need the WISDOM of the experts in your life.

If you have a friend who is boy-crazy and you are worried about her, sit down first and talk the situation through with an adult. Go on a wisdom-gathering quest. Be sure the advice you are about to give that friend on the boy-crazy train is sound.

Before we move on, how about another peek at my (Suzy's) cry for help: "I needed my friends to step up and *rescue* me."

If my first mistake in the above sentence was believing that my friends were ready to be my trusted advisors, the second was believing they were able to rescue me. No one can rescue another person. Boy, is this an important life lesson to learn!

Oh, we can rescue other people from physical harm. My little cousin fell into the swimming pool when he was only a toddler. I happened to be the nearest one to him, so on that day I got to play the role of hero. I saved his life! But this kind of rescue only works when there are swimming pools, fires, and speeding cars involved. When we are talking about people choosing to behave in ways that are dangerous, it's not as simple as jumping into a pool and pulling someone out.

How to Help a Boy-Crazy Friend

There are three routes you can take with a friend who is on such a runaway boy-crazy train that you can see a big fiery crash in her near future. Which one do you think would work most effectively? Maybe you can circle it.

1 **You can sit back and do nothing.** This is tempting. If you do nothing you can pretend you are surprised when the crash happens. The problem with this is the Bible says if we know there is something good we should do, but we fail to do it…we sin (James 4:17). When we see trouble coming, whether it's heading straight for a best friend or someone we don't even like very much, we should warn them. Silence doesn't work because it makes us the guilty party.

2 **You can try to handle the problem on your own.** Sometimes this is better than doing nothing, and I'll be the first to admit I've met some wise Secret Keeper Girls out there on the road! A lot of you girls impress me. Science usually aligns well with truth,

though, and science says our problem-solving skills need a lot of help for the first 25 years of our lives. That's a long time. This is why the Bible tells us that two are better than one.

3 **You can get the experts involved.** Even though we are both grown up and fully wise (yeah, right), we run every major decision and confrontation past someone else equally grown-up and wise! (Often we use each other for this—Dannah asking Suzy for advice or Suzy asking Dannah.) This is the best course of action. Two are way better than one. Even a king needs trusted advisors. Why wouldn't you and I?

Really
THINK ABOUT IT!

Go to Meditation #5 in Part 2. It's titled "Who Does God Want Me to Ask for Advice About Boys?"

Before you talk to that boy-crazy friend of yours, sit down and have an ice-cream sundae (no one ever outgrows ice cream) with someone who is loaded with wisdom. Ask a lot of questions. Form a plan. Pray. Your older, wiser friend might just advise you, or they may get involved like Dannah's mom did. But let them help. (P.S.—this sitting-down-for-ice-cream thing even works if it's not a friend who is on the runaway boy-crazy train, but *you*. We recommend chocolate-chip mint!)

get some advice with ice cream

BOY CRAZY?

What Should I Do While I'm Waiting to Date?

What should you do while you're waiting to date?

Well…what are you good at? The secret lies in the answer to that question. Among the readers of this book are great dancers, singers, musicians, actresses, debaters, thinkers, teachers, writers, caregivers, animal trainers…the list goes on and on.

My (Suzy's) family says I'm good at everything. They are kind, and they are wrong. I don't know why they would make this claim because they were the ones I last went bowling with. My daughter Marie and I were tied for last place, and I don't like losing.

I became very serious. Tiptoeing toward the line for my last roll—I only needed two pins to win—I felt it before I saw it. The ball had become stuck, lodged on my swelling right thumb. (It was like Jack Horner's nightmare all over again. I stuck in my thumb and pulled out…a bowling ball!) Of course the bowling ball and my swollen thumb were no match for the sheer speed and power of my bowling game. My arm was moving fast enough for a powerful strike, and when that ball dislodged itself from my thumb it went flying (almost) straight up in the air. Almost, you ask? Yes, it was at just enough of an angle that it landed right next to the man who was bowling in the lane next to me. My oldest daughter then pronounced, "Mom, that is the most unathletic thing I have ever seen you do."

I'm not good at bowling. There are other gifts that showed up in my childhood, however, that I wish I had spent time perfecting. If only I could take back the endless hours I spent watching horrible television shows simply because I thought there was a cute boy on the screen. If only I could get back all of the hours I spent poring over silly celebrity magazines and cutting out pictures for my locker door. Could I have been a professional golfer? Played college basketball? Made my living playing drums in a band? It's likely I could have.

If you want to be great at something (and who doesn't want to be great?) it's going to take a little work on your part. One of my favorite writers says it's going to take you about 10,000 hours to become truly great at something! That piano you like to play? One hour of practice is only going to take you 1/10,000 of the way to playing on the big stage. You know that obsession with basketball and how you are hoping to play in college? Yep, 10,000 hours of dribbling and shooting free throws should do it. Is Broadway in your future? Maybe after you've spent 10,000 hours with your voice coach and in play rehearsals. It's not easy to be excellent. It's easy to do nothing.

10,000 hours? no kidding

10,000!

I was a pro at doing nothing! TV was my specialty. Let's look at a few days of my life as recorded in my diary...

January 12—Nothing happened today. I came home and watched TV.

February 6—Mom is starting to get on my case about watching too much TV. I think she is crazy. I like TV and won't give it up.

April 13—Jammy and me were gonna go to a movie but I had a crummy piano lesson. So Jammy and Irina went bowling and Gretch and I were stuck at home. It all got better when TV came on. Good medicine.

No matter what day that diary opens to, the reader will get an eyeful of TV stars and shows. I watched TV—10,000 hours. I was an expert for sure.

There will never be a time in your life when you'll have so many free hours available to you as right now. You don't have bills to pay, a house to clean, or a job. Don't be distracted by Facebook. Learn something.

If you were to spend just ten hours per week (that's a couple of hours per day) pursuing something you were good at and loved to do, you could someday be an expert. What would you love to do? Mountain climbing, sailing, gymnastics, skating, singing, reading, writing, dance, bug collecting, videography, web design, animal training, painting…! You can do anything with all this time.

How to Become an Expert

Need some help figuring out what you might like to become an expert in? Here are some steps you can take toward excellence.

1 **If you don't already know what you like, try new things!** Accept new challenges, take classes, join a team, audition for a play. Find out where you excel, because I guarantee you are a natural at...something! A few years ago I (Dannah) took up tennis. I really enjoyed it but I didn't get good fast. At least, not as fast as I wanted. I'm probably never going to be a great tennis player, but it was good to try. At almost the same time, I went back to an old love: horseback riding. Now this I'm good at! And my gift returned really quickly. Trying doesn't always mean success, but when you keep trying you'll land on something you love.

2 **Get a coach.** Once you know what you love and where you have skill, begin to put in your 10,000 hours. Even though I (Suzy) didn't start playing drums until I was an adult, I found a drum teacher right away. I took lessons from three different drummers, each able to teach me new things. One of my teachers was a student in our youth group! I built a drum room in the basement, and my poor husband has spent a lot of hours having to listen to those drums through the walls of our house. I still have a ways to go, but I'm not done! I've learned enough to play in coffee shops and arenas; I've played drums on three CDs and for signed artists.

put in your 10,000 hours

3 **Practice both alone and in front of a crowd.** My (Suzy's) daughters had never played basketball before their adoption into our sports-crazed little family. Turns out they are both athletically inclined! So they entered their first year of basketball practice needing to learn some skills and gain a lot of knowledge about the game, but they were up for the challenge. Until the first game, that is. Suddenly the warm-ups we had practiced, those passing drills and layups, were being performed in front of a crowd. What if everyone was looking? Well, it turns out everyone will be looking if you compete, perform, or produce something! It's good to get used to a crowd of onlookers now. When you were little you used to say, "Mommy! Mommy! Daddy! Watch me!" Start saying that again.

4 **Turn off the TV and the computer.** Isn't it amazing how time flies when we watch three episodes of (name your favorite show) in a row? Or when you get on Facebook and look at things people say that aren't important? (If you're not on Facebook yet, wait! It's a real time waster.) TV and social media are fun, but time spent on them can easily become time wasted. Instead, spend time with friends, siblings, or your parents. Invite them to do your favorite things with you. Give them lessons for fun. Take pictures and laugh as they try to do a ballet leap or dribble a soccer ball. Dad attempting a round-off cartwheel? Priceless! Teaching what we love to do is another way of learning. It helps us build relationship and communication skills. It's part of the 10,000 hours, and it's fun!

Dad doing a round-off cartwheel? Call 911.

5 **Make a schedule.** It's unusual at your age to be making schedules, but remember, we're not going for normal here! It doesn't have to be minute by minute, but write out goals like "I want to spend one hour every day working on my game (my voice, my drawings, whatever that special thing is)." Limit the time spent doing things like TV or talking on the phone. And read more! Did you know that reading activates parts of your brain, causing it to grow?

What Should I Do While I'm Waiting to Date?

THINK ABOUT IT

How did you spend your 57,600 seconds yesterday? Write down all of the activities you can remember:

_____

_____

_____

_____

_____

_____

_____

_____

_____

_____

_____

_____

Those same parts of your brain go to sleep when you watch television. So put some reading time in that daily schedule too.

My diary is filled with days where the first thought I recorded was, "Today was so boring!" Here's a little something for you scientifically minded girls—the 24 hours we call a day are "values-neutral." This means they are neither good nor bad. They are not exciting or boring. They are only what we make of them. A day cannot be boring. But we, as human beings, can be bored. The choice is up to us. We're awake about 16 hours of each day. This breaks down to 960 minutes or 57,600 seconds! That's a lot of time we have available.

Here's to you, Secret Keeper Girl! You have been fearfully and wonderfully created. God's workmanship in you is perfect—that means he made you well! And he has plans for you. He thinks about you all the time. This truth can all be found in Psalm 139. One of these days, those plans may include a date, then a boyfriend, then a husband. Since we're not ready for that just yet, here's to the awesomely crafted girl who has so many interests and skills to discover. Here's to the girl who has so many wonderful things to create. Here's to *you* finding out exactly how God has created you and becoming his rock star.

Really THINK ABOUT IT!

Go to Meditation #6 in Part 2. It's titled "What Does God Want Me to Do with My 'Single Years'?"

On your mark! Get set!

ROCK OUT!

Part 2

What **God Says** About **Boys**— Bible Study

Getting Ready to DIG IN to Bible Study

The front half of this book is full of stories and wisdom. But that's not enough. You have to dig for the rest of this treasure yourself. The Bible is God's love letter to...*you*! So roll up your sleeves and get ready to build on that foundation of yours. Jesus said it himself in Matthew 7:24-25—if we put his words into practice (if we are *doers*) we are building a house so strong that even the storms of life cannot take us down.

The Bible studies in the Secret Keeper Girl Series use the powerful skill of *meditation*. So, before you get into the great subject of relating to boys, let's take a little time to learn about meditation.

What Is Meditation?

Well, you might think it's some crazy, weird thing you do while sitting cross-legged in a yoga position and humming. That's not true at all. That kind of meditation is just a sad fake of God's original. Let's take a look at what God says meditation should be.

Some Christians are really rigid about studying, studying, studying the Bible!

Some Christians are so consumed with praying all the time, they never study!

STUDIER

PRAY-ER

The risk for the studier is that her faith gets stuck in her head. She never has the *heart* to follow God because she is always arguing about or defending what she *thinks* about God.

The risk for the pray-er is that her faith is all about her heart. She makes decisions to follow God based on how she *feels* and forgets to think about what he has already told her in his written Word. (God will never ask you to do something that disagrees with the Bible.)

But then there's a third type of person. A meditator studies the Bible and then asks God to help her understand it while she prays. A wise pastor once told me (Dannah) that meditation is what happens when studying and praying crash into each other!

MEDITATOR

We want to teach you to meditate. You don't need a yoga mat! But you do need these things:

1. Your Bible. (You won't need to use it a lot, but that's because we're keeping this Bible study simple. All the verses you'll need are printed right in this book. But we want you to get in the habit of having your very own treasured Bible on hand.)

2. This copy of the Secret Keeper Girl Series book *A Girl's Guide to Understanding Boys*!

3. Some colored markers or pencils.

These are your meditation tools. Got 'em? Okay. Let's go.

What Does God Say About Boys?

Unless you go to an all girls' school, chances are you rub shoulders with the smellier portion of humanity every day. So we're really going to start a Bible study by proclaiming the odiferous (look it up if you need to) nature of boys? Well, we may as well get the truth out of the way. This may surprise you, but the truth is not that boys are smellier. The truth is that girls have more sensitive scent receptors. The truth is, girls are more concerned with hygiene than boys are. Put those two truths together and boys have the unfortunate distinction of being considered the smellier of the two genders.

DIG IN by Studying

The reality? God has made men and women to be equal but different. Take a look at this verse:

> "There is no longer Jew or Gentile, slave or free, male and female. For you are all one in Christ Jesus" (Galatians 3:28).

When you read that verse, do you think boys have been made better or higher than girls? Do you think God loves one gender more than the other? When Paul wrote this letter to the church, Gentiles (non-Jews), slaves, and women were not allowed to participate in church services. Paul was making a bold new statement about Jesus and his church.

HINT:
Not +, not −, but =
in God's Kingdom.

All people are _____.

"Equal" and "the same" are not the same things, though. Circle the words or phrases below that best describe you.

I talk a lot	I don't use many words
I can do two things at once	I can only do one thing at a time
I love words	I love math
I cry easily	I don't cry often

The words on the left would typically describe the way God created a female brain. The words on the right would be more like the way a boy's brain was created. Of course God created us each to be unique, so there are girls who are great at math and boys who talk way too much! Generally speaking, though, our brains are different in structure.

Here is the thing about being different—we need to be careful we don't think different means *better, worse,* or *wrong.* Paul has already warned us in Galatians that our differences don't matter in God's kingdom. Let's look at these three case studies to understand the concept even better.

1 Case study #1: Maggie and Carter. Maggie and Carter are in the same fourth-grade class. The student with the highest grade-point average gets to help the teacher plan the last-day-of-school activities. This is a tradition in Mrs. Castle's homeroom, and students compete hard all year long to win the honor. Maggie and Carter have ended up in a tie. Both have a 96 percent average. Maggie's reading scores are the highest in the class, while Carter's science scores are the highest. Carter has appealed to Mrs. Castle that he should win the honor of co-planner for the last day of school since science is more important than reading. Based on Galatians 3:28, what would you say to Carter and Maggie? Is being good at science better than being good at reading?

_____

_____

_____

_____

2 **Case study #2: Erin and Lucas.** Erin and Lucas have both been given recess detention for a week, though their "crimes" are not the same. Lucas hit another boy, causing a bloody nose. The boys were fighting over who was up next in their game of kickball. Erin passed a note to a new girl that read, "No one here likes you." Erin is insisting to Mrs. Castle that since she didn't write the note (Taylor did) and because hitting someone is much worse than passing a note, her punishment should be less than Lucas's. Based on Galatians 3:28, what would you say to Erin and Lucas? Is a bully who hits someone worse than a bully who passes a mean note?

_____

_____

_____

_____

3 **Case study #3: Nick and Alexis.** Yesterday a volunteer from the local pet shelter presented a slide show about animal cruelty. She said the shelter has too many animals and too few cages, and she encouraged students to start a campaign to raise money for the shelter so fewer dogs and cats would suffer. Alexis collected $200 by the end of the day and plans to collect through the end of the week. Nick has politely refused to give money to Alexis, saying he prefers to give money to causes that help people. Alexis has come to Mrs. Castle in tears, insisting that Nick has no heart. She will never do anything for him again. What would you say to Alexis and Nick based on Galatians 3:28? Is Nick wrong for not feeling greater compassion for shelter animals whose lives are in danger?

DIFFERENT!

_____

_____

_____

_____

_____

_____

_____

_____

Different certainly is not better, worse, or wrong. One of the most important things we can realize as we spend time with the boys in our lives, no matter how old or young they may be, is that God designed these differences on purpose.

How about a little art to round out the day? As you read the verses below, which are found in the Bible's account of creation, draw a picture for the jobs given to men and the jobs given to women. Pay attention to details as you draw.

Here's what God said to the man, both before and after he sinned. Draw a picture that represents this in the BOYS box.

15 The LORD God placed the man in the Garden of Eden to tend and watch over it. **16** But the LORD God warned him, "You may freely eat the fruit of every tree in the garden—**17** except the tree of the knowledge of good and evil. If you eat its fruit, you are sure to die."

18 Then the LORD God said, "It is not good for the man to be alone. I will make a helper who is just right for him."

19 So the LORD God formed from the ground all the wild animals and all the birds of the sky. He brought them to the man to see what he would call them, and the man chose a name for each one (Genesis 2:15-19).

And...

17 "Since you listened to your wife and ate from the tree whose fruit I commanded you not to eat, the ground is cursed because of you. All your life you will struggle to scratch a living from it. **18** It will grow thorns and thistles for you, though you will eat of its grains" (Genesis 3:17-18).

Did you draw pictures of boys building things, making things, growing food, hunting, fishing, farming? It's natural for a boy to like to build things, make things grow, hunt, fish, farm, and produce things that feed a family. But now God has told him these things will frustrate him. This world is not going to cooperate with him.

Here's what God said to the woman, both before and after she sinned. Draw a picture that represents this in the GIRLS box.

 The LORD God said, "It is not good

for the man to be alone. I will make a

helper who is just right for him"

(Genesis 2:18).

 And...

"I will sharpen the pain of your pregnancy,

and in pain you will give birth.

And you will desire to control your husband,

but he will rule over you"

(Genesis 3:16).

Maybe you drew pictures of girls caring for babies, bringing water to the farmer, or caring for the house. It's natural for a girl to feel compassion and want to nurture those who are smaller and weaker. We want to be able, reliable, strong, smart, and beautiful all at the same time. But now God has told us these desires will be frustrating too. One of the jobs we've been given is to help others grow, rule, and shine...but others may not want to cooperate!

Do you see the key point in these verses? What we were created to do is now very difficult for us. But it's been our choosing, so we have to live with it. And there is super good news! Sin may have started the boys-vs.-girls war, but Jesus came to wipe that out.

GIRLS

S.G.N.

Super Good News!

What Does God Say About Boys?

Remember Galatians 3:28? Unscramble it below, looking back at it if you have to (but try not to):

Rethe si on grenlo Jwe ro Gtenlie,

Isvae ro eefr, lame dna mafeel.

Fro uyo rea lal neo ni Cthsir Jsseu.

_ _ _ _ _   _ _   _ _   _ _ _ _ _   _ _

_ _   _ _   _ _ _ _ _ _ ,

_ _ _ _ _   _ _   _ _ _ _ ,

_ _ _ _   _ _ _   _ _ _ _ _ .

_ _ _   _ _ _ _   _ _ _   _ _ _

_ _   _ _ _ _ _ _   _ _ _ _ .

You see, this thing called sin has been nothing but a human-relationship wrecker from the beginning. Where people were meant to protect one another, sin causes them to harm one another. Where people were supposed to lead side by side, sin causes one to rise up in power and force the other person to bow down. Where God created a rainbow of skin colors, sin has led people to put others in a lower or higher place based on color. But as we see in Galatians, Jesus takes everything we invited sin to mess up and makes it all right again. No race wars anymore—there is no black or white in Jesus. Both are the same. No slavery anymore—all people are set free in Jesus. And no boys vs. girls. Both are equal in God's kingdom. Boys may not be so gross after all...

Reach Up to Talk to GOD

Dear Jesus,

Thank you for your creation. It's awesome. Not only all the beautiful things you made to look at, but also all the people. Thank you for making both male and female. I have to confess that sometimes boys just frustrate me! Still, I'm seeing that you created them fearfully and wonderfully. I'm seeing it's just as hard to be a boy as it is to be a girl. Sin has made things difficult for all of us. Lord, help me to understand Galatians 3:28. Help me think straight when I begin to believe boys are better than girls, because that makes me feel _____. Correct my thinking when I begin to believe girls are better than boys because that makes me act _____. And remind me every day that "different" is not the same thing as "wrong." Sin messed everything up in this world, but Jesus, you are putting everything back in its proper place. Today, remind me that _____ is more than just a cute boy. Show me how you view _____ as more than an irritating boy. Let me know that _____ is not better than me because he can run faster or solve problems that stump me. Help me to know that _____ is not heartless—he just doesn't show as much emotion as my girlfriends do. Remind me that in your creation, Jesus, different can even be good!

In Jesus' Name,

_____

(Sign here)

What Does God Say About Being Boy-Crazy?

Y ou stayed up too late last night again. You were just reading a book, and reading is good for you, right? Sure it is! It builds brain cells and stimulates your imagination. It helps you to learn problem-solving skills and it builds empathy for others—that means it's an activity that teaches you to have compassion. That's all-star stuff right there! But it's been happening a lot, and you missed your bus because you didn't hear your alarm clock go off. And yesterday you fell asleep in class.

"This is the third time this week," your mom reminds you as she drives you to school. "If it happens again I'm going to start charging you a taxi fare."

"I know, Mom. I already told you I'm sorry. It won't happen again." You cross your arms and stare out the window. Why is it suddenly so irritating to be in the car with her? Yesterday after school she kept asking all those questions about your school day. *What did you learn? Who did you eat lunch with? How do you like your new teacher? Did you have a chance to clean your locker yet? Do you have any homework?* It's funny how irritating those questions can be in the car, but you still can't fall asleep at night unless she tucks you in and you've both kissed Boomer the Bear goodnight. It's been your bedtime ritual since you were three.

Maybe, you think, *if I could just hang out at Gabi's house this weekend and get to be part of a normal family for a change.* Gabi has a huge house, only one little brother, and she pretty much gets to do whatever she wants. It would be kind of nice to stay up late and not be told to turn out the lights. It might be nice to eat food in bed (which you aren't allowed to do) and watch TV. You don't have a TV in your bedroom.

When you get to Gabi's you find out you're not the only one spending the night. Three other girls are there too. It's kind of embarrassing that you brought Boomer the Bear, but you've never spent a night without him. The girls say he's cute, so it seems okay. You swim, play tag among the giant oak trees in Gabi's backyard, and wolf down burgers that her dad has cooked on the grill. After bringing enough junk food to feed an army up to Gabi's room, the girls announce it's time for girl talk. You're thinking the mall, cute clothes, a new song by your favorite band...but the girls have the school directory out and they are talking about the boys in your class. "Who should we call first?" Gabi grins. The girls giggle and you squeeze Boomer tight.

DIG IN by Studying

Check out what Ephesians 4:17-18 says:

17 And so I insist—and God backs me up on this—that there be no going along with the crowd, the empty-headed, mindless crowd. **18** They've refused for so long to deal with God that they've lost touch not only with God but with reality itself. They can't think straight anymore (MSG).

Now dig into this crossword puzzle.

SKG
Puzzle Craze

For puzzle answers go to page 104.

ACROSS

3. How long has the crowd refused to follow God?
5. This word is a partner to empty-headed.
7. How the crowd can no longer think

DOWN

1. Who does the opposite of what is weird?
2. What book of the Bible is this verse found in?
4. The crowd does not live in this.
6. God says, "I _____" on this.
8. The crowd will not obey him.
9. The crowd is out of _____.

This is not the only verse where God insists that we are set apart for him. Do you know what the word for "set apart" is in the Bible? It's "*holy.*" When he says something is *holy*, it means he has set it apart for his own use, enjoyment, pleasure, or service. It's different than everything else. **Let's take a look at 1 Peter 2:9-12:**

9 But you are not like that, for you are a chosen people. You are royal priests, a holy nation, God's very own possession. As a result, you can show others the goodness of God, for he called you out of the <u>darkness</u> into his wonderful light. **10** "Once you had no identity as a people; now you are God's people. Once you received no mercy; now you have received God's mercy." **11** Dear friends, I warn you as "temporary residents and foreigners" to keep away from worldly desires that wage war against your very souls. **12** Be careful to live properly among your unbelieving neighbors. Then even if they accuse you of doing wrong, they will see your honorable behavior, and they will give honor to God when he judges the world.

You and both of us have been set apart for God. We are his very own possessions! But don't think of possessions in the same way you might think of your iPod or your bike. We belong to God as his family, his children, and his friends. If you did the Bible study in the book *A Girl's Guide to Best Friends and Mean Girls*, you'll remember that *Jesus chose you*! This verse in 1 Peter says the same thing. We are not his because he won a contest or found us on a sales rack. We belong to him because he paid a high price for us. Jesus paid for us, for our freedom from sin and death, with his life. Since we belong to him, he insists that we live like we are part of his family, not the normal way everyone else lives.

Look Inside Yourself

♡ ♡ ♡

Cattie Crowd is a normal girl. That's not the same thing as saying she is "bad." She's doing what comes natural for a girl your age. In fact, fill in all the blanks for what is normal for girls your age. But check out the underlined word in verse 9 of 1 Peter 2. Cattie and the crowd are walking in:

CATTIE CROWD

_____.

❀ It is normal for Cattie to look at:

_____

_____

❀ Cattie talks about

_____

_____

❀ Cattie listens to:

_____

_____

❀ Cattie loves:

_____

_____

❀ Cattie likes to go:

_____

_____

Now, take time to fill in the blanks for "It's ME!" Instead of writing what is normal, write what kind of behaviors will make you special and "set apart" for God's kingdom! (Remember from earlier in the book, letting God have the first and last word means you'll stick out and look a little crazy from time to time! That's a good thing!)

IT'S ME!

🦋 My eyes will be set apart if I look at:

_____

_____.

🦋 I can be different if I talk about:

_____

_____.

🦋 My ears will be set apart if I listen to:

_____

_____.

🦋 I'll be set apart if I love:

_____

_____.

🦋 I can bless God by going:

_____

_____.

What Does God Say About Being Boy-Crazy?

It is not easy to be special and set apart. It's far more natural to be normal, but you can do it. In fact, here's how we know you can do it.

TRY THIS!

Stand up right now and close your eyes. (Well, in a moment. After you read the next three sentences.) Now proceed (very carefully) to your family's washing machine. See if you can get there without opening your eyes at all. Then open your eyes and walk back to your copy of *A Girl's Guide to Understanding Boys.*

We'll bet you walked back to your Bible study book (with your eyes wide open) much more quickly than you walked to that washing machine! That's because your eyes were open. You could see the light!

Unscramble the mixed-up words:

Spiritually, you used to walk in darkness, but God has called you

out into his DWFEORNLU GILTH: _____

_____ ! Peter says this world is not our home.

He says we are YTPROMAER _____ residents and

OSFRINGERE _____. What is "normal" doesn't

apply to us. The darkness is not supposed to be what we walk in.

Not where we come from! And the bonus is, when we walk in the

light, we can show others the SSOOGDNE _____

of God!

Reach Up to Talk to GOD

Hi, God!

I have to confess I have spent a lot of time thinking about being normal, or fitting in. But I see now that you have called me to be set apart...or special. I need to get used to thinking about how I can do that. I'm going to take a minute right now to practice. *(Spend some time thinking about ways to be set apart instead of chasing the same things every other girl is chasing.)* Okay, God, I've come up with a couple of new things I can focus on instead of popularity, boys, attention, or approval. One is _____ and the other is _____.

The Bible says if I do this I'll lead others to see your goodness. I want to ask for this to happen, especially for my friends _____ and _____. Thank you! I'm excited about being part of your family and being, well, a little different!

In Jesus' Name,

_____

(Sign here)

Who Does God Say Gets to Decide When I Start to Date?

The rumor is spreading like a wildfire throughout the school. It's finally happened. The first couple from the class of Two-Thousand-Never (how many years till you're a high-school senior?) has made its epic appearance. Spencer and Kate. The names may as well be Hollywood royalty. Spencer and Kate are dating!

"I heard Spencer gave Kate a necklace."

"I thought she liked Nelson."

"Yeah, me too."

The crowds part as the royal couple walks from art class to recess, Spencer with his buds and Kate with her BFFs. The boys head off to play kickball. The girls rush to the swings. Throughout recess Spencer and Kate never even glance at one another. One note ("You look pretty") is passed before the end of the day, but Kate's parents find it that night, and by morning the relationship is over. Spencer and Kate, alas, have learned they are _not yet allowed_ to date. It seems to be okay, though. Spencer is sliding into third on the baseball diamond and Kate is laughing as she plays four square.

As you begin to see "dating" relationships pop up among your classmates, you will notice a rapid-fire pace of beginnings and endings. Why do these relationships pop up so fast and end so quickly? It has a lot to do with the very definition of dating, a definition you'll find in a dictionary but not in the Bible. The concept of dating was not present in either Old or New Testaments. There are, however, a couple of clues in the sentences above that we can address by looking into God's Word.

Write the three underlined words from the previous page in the blanks below:

_____   _____ AND

_____

DIG IN by Studying

Let's look at "not yet" through the eyes of 1 Corinthians 13:11-12.

11 When I was a child, I spoke and thought and reasoned as a child. But when I grew up, I put away childish things. **12** Now we see things imperfectly like puzzling reflections in a mirror, but then we will see everything with perfect clarity. All that I know now is partial and incomplete, but then I will know everything completely, just as God now knows me completely.

Have you ever babysat or helped to take care of a little cousin? If you have, you've noticed that little ones don't see things the same way you do. For instance, fill out this little chart:

	I'd use it to:	A toddler would use it to:
An iPhone	_____	_____
A book	_____	_____
A Coke	_____	_____

You can probably see our point. A little child does not arrive in this world with the instruction manual already memorized! She has to be taught. Some things are too valuable to put into her hands for years. She will just ruin them until she is ready to use them correctly.

Life can be the same way. You won't be driving alone until you are at least 16. Voting comes at age 18. Rental-car companies won't rent to anyone under 22. The president of the United States must be 35 years old...that sounds ancient, doesn't it? But these age limits have a reason. According to Paul, who wrote the book of 1 Corinthians, it's because children speak, think, and reason like

_____. You're not really a child, but you're not an adult yet either.

The other day my friend's five-year-old was playing a game with me after church. He would run to the drinking fountain and soak his shirt with water (sounds fun, right?) and then he would run up to me and say, "Feel my shirt!" I would and he would squeal with delight, "It's wet! I tricked you! I tricked you!" Jack thought I wouldn't know his shirt was wet unless I touched it. But I knew! Wet fabric is much darker than dry fabric. It clings to the body. But little Jack doesn't see with this clarity yet. He can't see it. *Not. Yet.*

SKG
Puzzle Craze

Now let's look at the word "allowed" through the eyes of Ephesians 6:1-3:

1 Children, obey your parents because you belong to the Lord, for this is the right thing to do.

2 "Honor your father and mother." This is the first commandment with a promise: **3** If you honor your father and mother, "things will go well for you, and you will have a long life on the earth."

What does it mean to you to "honor" someone? That's an important question. Does it just mean to obey, or is there more to it? You bet there's more to it! There are all kinds of things we will obey simply because they are right, or because we are afraid not to obey. See if you can find some of them in this double puzzle. Unscramble each of the clue words. Take the letters that appear in circled boxes and unscramble them for the final message. We've underlined the first letter of each word for you.

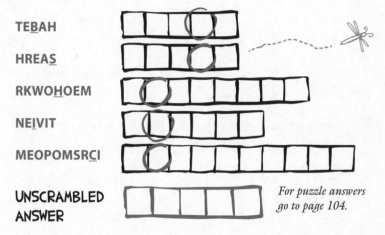

TE<u>B</u>AH

HREA<u>S</u>

RKWO<u>H</u>OEM

NE<u>I</u>VIT

MEOPOMSR<u>C</u>I

UNSCRAMBLED ANSWER

For puzzle answers go to page 104.

The Hebrew word "honor" means to "fix value to something." When something is "fixed," it is going to stay where it is. In other words, when we honor our parents it's a matter of actually saying, "What they say goes. It's fixed!" If we honor our parents, we don't have permission to move beyond things until they say so. We aren't allowed.

Look Inside Yourself

So how much do I honor my mom and dad, or the other key adults in my life? Remember, we are not asking, "Do I obey?" We are totally supposed to obey, but here we are simply asking, "Do I think they have valuable things to teach me? When they talk to me about what is good and right, what is best to do...do I trust them, or do I roll my eyes?"

Here's a checklist so you can give yourself a basic score:

1. I study the way my parents suggest so I can get the most out of school.
☐ NEVER ☐ SOMETIMES ☐ ALWAYS

2. I let my parents have some say in who my friends are.
☐ NEVER ☐ SOMETIMES ☐ ALWAYS

3. I know what they think about when I can date and I honor that.
☐ NEVER ☐ SOMETIMES ☐ ALWAYS

4. I follow my parents' rules even if I'm at someone else's house.
☐ NEVER ☐ SOMETIMES ☐ ALWAYS

5. When I do mess up, I'm sure to tell my parents I'm sorry.
☐ NEVER ☐ SOMETIMES ☐ ALWAYS

6. The things I say about my parents to other people are positive and honoring.
☐ NEVER ☐ SOMETIMES ☐ ALWAYS

7. I ask my parents for advice before I make big decisions.
☐ NEVER ☐ SOMETIMES ☐ ALWAYS

8. I think my parents have a lot of wisdom.
☐ NEVER ☐ SOMETIMES ☐ ALWAYS

How did you do? You likely found some areas for improvement. We wrote the checklist that way on purpose. Look, not everyone has the same situation at home. Some of you have single parents, so that "s" was unnecessary on the word "parent." Grandparents may be raising you, or you could be the only Christian in your household. Your situation is unique. But God's Word is still firm on its insistence that you (and we, no matter how old we are) place great value on the things our parents say to us.

Most likely, your parents are going to say "*not allowed yet*" when it comes to dating, and this may continue for some time. How about moving some of those checkmarks into the "always" column and letting them protect you? It's okay for you to be a child for a little while yet!

Reach Up to Talk to GoD

𝒢od, you're my dad, right? And I'm your kid. I'm not ready to be a grown-up just yet. Before I grow up, I'd like to spend a few more years enjoying these things about being a kid: _____

_____

_____

_____.

There's plenty of time for grown-up things when I get there. I know that the people who love me are all about protecting me, and I know you've told me to honor and value them. I need to grow in this area, especially when I'm asked to

_____. But the Bible says I'll have a long life if I value the things they say. I'm going to work on that, God. I'm going to work on getting to know you so I can value what you say, and I'm going to work on honoring the following adults too: _____

_____.

Please teach me how to honor. Here's to long life!

Thank you,

_____

(Sign here)

How Does God Want Me to Act Around Boys?

There's no doubt about it. Nathan and Ben are the two coolest guys in your class. They are popular, have an awesome sense of fashion, are the best ones to have on your team for current-events contests, make everyone laugh during those corny classroom movies…and you have just witnessed them making Daniel cry. Daniel is kind of the opposite of Nathan and Ben. Daniel doesn't have many friends. He doesn't wear "cool" clothes, he smells like he might need to be introduced to deodorant, and he can't catch or throw a ball. Come to think of it, he can't even run from point A to point B without stumbling. It's not unusual for kids to make fun of him behind his back.

Now you have a choice to make. The other kids are patting Nathan and Ben on the back, telling them how funny and cool they are. If you step in you might be seen as uncool. Nathan and Ben might not like you. Even worse, the popular girls in your class may not like you. But you know what is right—you know what you would want someone to do if you were Daniel. Stepping into the circle of laughing classmates you…

1. Slap Nathan and Ben.

2. High-five Nathan and Ben.

3. Scream, "I don't like any of you!" at the entire group.

4. Calmly tell Nathan and Ben that what they did was not good, then go to find and help Daniel.

DIG IN by Studying Luke 10:25-37

25 One day an expert in religious law stood up to test Jesus by asking him this question: "Teacher, what should I do to inherit eternal life?" **26** Jesus replied, "What does the law of Moses say? How do you read it?" **27** The man answered, "'You must love the Lord your God with all your heart, all your soul, all your strength, and all your mind.' And, 'Love your neighbor as yourself.'" **28** "Right!" Jesus told him. "Do this and you will live!" **29** The man wanted to justify his actions, so he asked Jesus, "And who is my neighbor?"

30 Jesus replied with a story: "A Jewish man was traveling on a trip from Jerusalem to Jericho, and he was attacked by bandits. They stripped him of his clothes, beat him up, and left him half dead beside the road. **31** By chance a priest came along. But when he saw the man lying there, he crossed to the other side of the road and passed him by.

Draw the bandits here.

Draw the priest here.

Draw the temple assistant here.

Draw the Samaritan here.

32 A Temple assistant walked over and looked at him lying there, but he also passed by on the other side. **33** Then a despised Samaritan came along, and when he saw the man, he felt compassion for him. **34** Going over to him, the Samaritan soothed his wounds with olive oil and wine and bandaged them. Then he put the man on his own donkey and took him to an inn, where he took care of him. **35** The next day he handed the innkeeper two silver coins, telling him, 'Take care of this man. If his bill runs higher than this, I'll pay you the next time I'm here.' **36** Now which of these three would you say was a neighbor to the man who was attacked by bandits?" Jesus asked. **37** The man replied, "The one who showed him mercy." Then Jesus said, "Yes, now go and do the same."

How should I act around boys? The exact same way I act around all of my neighbors. Grab some markers, and let's apply some color to the story of the Good Samaritan. First, place a red heart around every instance of the word "love" and every loving action you see in the story above. Draw a yellow line through every unmerciful action you read about. In the margin draw the bandits, the priest, the Temple assistant (today this might be a worship leader or a children's pastor), and the Samaritan. Next to each drawing, write a word or two to describe how that person is *supposed* to act.

Guess what? If we circled the person acting the way they are "supposed" to act, the only one we could circle is the bandit! Robbers, by definition, rob people. They steal and cause harm. Go ahead and circle the bandit, but now let's look at the other three, who weren't exactly doing as expected.

1 The priest. The priest in Jesus' time was a little bit like a pastor today. He was responsible for leading Israel spiritually. His life was supposed to be an example for the people. He was to be holy, just like God. What did the priest do when he encountered the robbery victim? He _____ to the other side of the road. He thought he was doing the right thing. A priest who touched blood was considered unclean. Surely God wouldn't want him to break that law...or would he?

2 The Temple assistant. The assistant might be compared to anyone else who works in the church today. He was called to God's work, making a living by helping others to perform their acts of worship. He was likely traveling this road from Jericho to Jerusalem on his way to work! He came one step closer to helping than the priest did. He actually _____... but then he, too, crossed the road and went on his way.

3 The Samaritan. Samaritans were from the northern part of Israel. They were often of mixed Jewish and Gentile blood and had a reputation for worshiping pagan gods. The southern part of Israel had remained much purer, and the Jews there more or less hated Samaritans for their unfaithfulness to God. A Samaritan who found a dying Jew would be expected to rejoice over his enemy's misfortune. But this Samaritan didn't do what he was "supposed" to do. Instead, he did what Jesus now says is a model for how we should treat other people—no matter who they are.

For puzzle answers go to page 104.

SKG
Puzzle Craze

After you've run the maze, write down the six things the Samaritan did (see the drawings above) in order to help his wounded enemy/neighbor.

1. He _____ at his situation.

2. He _____ his wounds.

3. He put _____ on his sores.

4. He placed him on his own _____.

5. He took him to an _____ where he could rest and recover.

6. He _____ the entire bill.

Look Inside Yourself

The Bible doesn't have too much to say about how we are supposed to act around boys. Timothy is told to treat girls with absolute purity, as if they were his sisters (1 Timothy 5:2) and girls are told to care more about their inner qualities than about outward beauty. Nowhere does the Bible say, "Girls, this is how you should act when you are around boys." What the Bible is full of, however, are reminders of how we are to treat other people. *All* other people. Boys, girls, friends, enemies, older, younger, richer, or poorer—it has a lot to do with the clothes we wear.

12 Since God chose you to be the holy people he loves, you must clothe yourselves with tenderhearted mercy, kindness, humility, gentleness, and patience. 13 Make allowance for each other's faults, and forgive anyone who offends you. Remember, the Lord forgave you, so you must forgive others. 14 Above all, clothe yourselves with love, which binds us all together in perfect harmony.

15 And let the peace that comes from Christ rule in your hearts. For as members of one body you are called to live in peace. And always be thankful (Colossians 3:12-15).

How about your clothes? Are you wearing things like forgiveness, patience, and love? If you are, you'll be the same person no matter who you are with. You'll stand up to Nathan and Ben no matter how cool they are. You'll chase down Daniel and let him know that you'll be his friend. And one of the best things of all…you won't have to make a bunch of noise to be noticed. People really like these Colossian clothes!

Write God a quick note here. Talk with him in your note about how well (or poorly) you are doing in dressing yourself in each of the items mentioned in Colossians 3.

A Girl's Guide to Understanding Boys

Here's a reminder checklist and a question to help you with each item.

- ☐ **A tender heart**—Do I feel bad when I see others being hurt?
- ☐ **Kindness**—Do I offer kindness, or am I the one who bullies?
- ☐ **Humility**—Do I have to be the center of attention?
- ☐ **Gentleness**—Am I too harsh with my looks or my words?
- ☐ **Patience**—Do I roll my eyes when things don't go my way or take too long?
- ☐ **Forgiveness**—How long do I stay mad?
- ☐ **Love**—Would I stop and take care of my enemy?

Reach Up to Talk to GOD

Dear Jesus,

I have to confess, sometimes I think if I don't get a little loud and crazy maybe no one will ever notice me. Now I'm thinking about how your goal wasn't to be noticed, but to notice others. I want to be like you. Honestly, I've been noticing several people who are lonely or hurting at school, like _____ and _____. I can tell they are hurting because _____ _____. I know you want me to treat all people with the same compassion, kindness, humility, patience, and love you do. I want to give up my desire to be noticed. Instead, I want to be like you and learn to notice others.

_____

(Sign here)

Who Does God Want Me to Ask for Advice About Boys?

Meet me after class behind the big cement tubes on the playground.

Wow. Something big must be up if your BFF is inviting you to meet by the playground tubes. This is your top-secret, all-things-BFF meeting place. This is where you found out her family had invited you to go to Disney World with them last year. This is where you told your BFF about Grandma's cancer and she prayed for you. This meeting ground is saved for the biggies and you both know it…

"Look what Devin gave me!" she squeals as you approach the tubes after class. She is holding up a little bracelet with blue, red, and diamond-like stones and grinning from ear to ear. She can't quit squealing.

"What is that?" you ask.

"Duh! It's a bracelet!" she says. "He asked me to be his girlfriend."

"I thought you weren't allowed to have a boyfriend," you say slowly. This feels funny.

"Yeah. I'm not going to tell my parents." She pauses, then squeals again. "Isn't this awesome! Do you like him? Do you think we're a perfect couple?"

"Uh, yeah. I'm...it's great." Why do you feel like there are cameras and microphones in the playground tubes recording your every word? Why do you feel uneasy? Why did you just say, "It's great?" This isn't great at all.

DIG IN by Studying Proverbs 11:14; 12:15; 15:22; 16:20; 19:20

Check out these verses from Proverbs about asking for advice. Did you know Proverbs is called the book of wisdom? True story!

"Without wise leadership, a nation falls; there is safety in having many advisers" (Proverbs 11:14).

"Fools think their own way is right, but the wise listen to others" (Proverbs 12:15).

"Plans go wrong for lack of advice; many advisers bring success" (Proverbs 15:22).

"Those who listen to instruction will prosper; those who trust the Lord will be joyful" (Proverbs 16:20).

"Get all the advice and instruction you can, so you will be wise the rest of your life" (Proverbs 19:20).

A lot of the advice that we give you in this book is kind of funny. Why? Because we sometimes ask you to live in ways that we did not. Believe it or not, this is wisdom. We know we should have done things differently.

When we didn't ask for advice from older, wiser people, we were unprepared. We just did what we thought was right. But both of us have experienced a lot of heartache and troubles because of following our own thinking instead of God's. When we don't ask for advice and just do what we think is right…things don't go so well. Circle every instance of the word "advice" or "instruction" in the verses from Proverbs above. Now see if you can solve the puzzle below:

SKG
Puzzle Craze

_____ _____ _____

_____ _____ __ _____

_____ _____ , _____

_____ _____ _____ _____

_____ _____ !

The w + 👁 👁 person will list + 10

to ad + 🗜, ma + 👑 her

w + 👁 👁 and sure 2 👶-ceed!

For puzzle answers go to page 104.

No matter how smart you are, even if one day you run a company or an entire country, you will seek advice if you want to be wise. Joshua was a very wise battle commander for God's army, but one time he decided to make a decision without asking God for advice. A nearby nation had heard Israel's God was going to deliver every other nation into Joshua's hands. So they dressed like they were from *very* far away and convinced Joshua to agree to a peace treaty with them. Though God had promised this nation to Joshua, he was never able to conquer it because he forgot to ask God for wisdom.

When you need to make a big decision, which of the following do you *always* do? Be super honest, because anything less won't help us learn!

☐ I always pray before a decision.

☐ I always tell an adult if there is a decision to be made.

☐ I always ask that adult for advice.

☐ I always look for wisdom from the Bible.

☐ I always ask friends what I should do.

☐ I always do the first thing that comes to mind.

☐ I always stay neutral and just let things work out naturally.

☐ I always do what makes others happy.

There is a big difference between the first four options and the last four. The first four, according to God's Word, should be done every time we need to make a big decision. This would not include a decision like, "Should I buy the $25 shoes or the $20 shirt?" That might be a call you can make on your own, or even with a friend. But in big decisions, like what to do with your BFF's news that she has a secret boyfriend, or how to talk to a friend who seems to be boy-crazed, the first four are the only way to come to a wise decision. In the space below, write down any of the first four options you did not put a check mark next to:

_____

_____

_____

_____

The second four options are not too safe. They are not necessarily sinful, but all four fall in the category of "foolish" according to Proverbs. This means they cannot lead us to good decisions. If you checked any of these four boxes, write them in the space below:

_____

_____

_____

_____

What do you do with your BFF's SECRET NEWS?

Fill in the blanks of this pledge below. It's simply a promise you can make to God that as you look for answers to big decisions or in handling big problems, you will go to good and healthy places for advice.

My Advice Pledge

I _____ (*insert your name*)

promise to seek wise counsel when I make decisions

and deal with problems. I will talk to you first,

God. And I will listen. I will talk to an adult. Here

are a couple of adults I feel comfortable talking to:

_____ and _____.

I will ask them for advice, and to help me search my Bible

for answers. In the past I have been asking ___friend,

___self, ___no one for advice. I need to add some extra

steps and I will. Proverbs 13:20 says if I walk with the

_____ I will grow _____, but if I associate

with _____ I will be in trouble. I am

going to walk with _____.

_____
(*Sign here*)

Dear God,

Reach Up to Talk to GOD

I'm ready to solve problems and make decisions the right way! I know I'm not ready to counsel my friends, but I have you, and there are wise adults in my life who can steer me the right way. It makes me feel _____ to involve you, the Bible, and adults in all of my decisions. It's ☐ new ☐ not new for me, but I'm behind this way of doing things _____ percent. Help me be 100 percent. I don't want to be wishy-washy when it comes to being wise!

_____

(Sign here)

*Dear Secret Keeper Girl, if you have a problem or decision eating away at you right now, go practice this right away! Take the problem to God, listen, and then go find an adult who will also listen and help you look for wisdom in the Bible. It's the best feeling in the world to share burdens with wise people!

What Does God Want Me to Do with my "Single Years"?

Okay, that seems like a crazy title for a tween girl to read. Some people would say you're not supposed to start considering yourself "single" until all your friends start to marry. We disagree. Your single years start now, friend. And they start with a dream...maybe like this one:

For as long as you can remember you've had this dream. When you close your eyes at night you can see it. The American flag is flying behind you. You are in an arena with thousands of people singing the national anthem. Tears stream down your face as your hands keep rising up to touch the gold medal around your neck. *Olympic champion*. No other words make your heart beat so quickly.

Today your friends are going to a movie starring the cutest movie star ever. They have been talking about it for weeks. But it's Saturday, and you get some of your best swimming in on Saturdays. There is a meet next weekend, and you are so close to setting your personal best record. And you really like your swim team too. The people are fun.

It's no contest for you. Today is a chance to get better. Today is a chance to get stronger in your best race. Today is one step closer to your lifelong dream. Your friends think you're crazy...this is going to be a really good movie. But you know what you want, and you know how to get there. You smile as you pack your bag for the YMCA.

DIG IN by Studying 1 Corinthians 9:24-27

Those who study the Bible for a living are certain the apostle Paul was a big sports fan. Oh yes, there were sports going on when Jesus was here on Earth. The first Olympic Games took place almost 800 years before his birth, as a matter of fact! Paul writes a lot about athletes and the work they need to put in before they can be considered excellent at their job. He doesn't use any flowery words. Becoming good at *anything* takes *hard* work!

 24 Don't you realize that in a race

everyone runs, but only one person

gets the prize? So run to win!

25 All athletes are disciplined in their

training. They do it to win a prize that

will fade away, but we do it for an

eternal prize. **26** So I run with purpose in

every step. I am not just shadowboxing.

27 I discipline my body like an athlete,

training it to do what it should.

Otherwise, I fear that after preaching to

others I myself might be disqualified

(1 Corinthians 9:24-27).

In this one little passage, Paul mentions two sports. Can you find them? _____ and _____ .

Of course sports aren't the only thing that takes hard work and dedication. If you and I are to become excellent at anything (and God has created us for excellence), it's going to take some work. Paul even trained for preaching the way an athlete might train.

Draw these symbols in the margins on page 94 whenever you see these words mentioned:

1. Next to anything about boxing draw the boxer.

2. Next to any mention of a prize or award draw the gold medal.

3. Next to anything about a race draw the runner.

4. Next to lines with "discipline" draw the stopwatch.

5. Next to mentions of training draw the strong arm.

6. Next to lines with "athlete" draw the Olympic jacket.

That's a lot of drawing you just had to do. Paul isn't messing around, and anyone who wants to become seriously good at something won't mess around either! Olympic athletes eat like they are serious…breakfast might be eight egg whites with spinach and cheese, oatmeal, or yogurt. That's an odd breakfast, but it's how they maintain those muscles. Olympic athletes train like they are serious…a 13-year-old Olympic hopeful may spend four hours a day in the gym after school and five hours on Saturdays.

What did you have for breakfast today? _____

_____

What Does God Want Me to Do With My "Single Years"?

What do you do during the four hours after school?

_____

_____

_____

We're not suggesting that you switch to protein bars for breakfast or spend four hours working out each day. Paul's main point here is that in order to become a dedicated follower of Jesus we have to work like an athlete. Hopefully, becoming a great follower of Jesus sounds like a fun challenge to you. As his follower, he has something unique planned for you because of the way he has created you and the way he has gifted you.

 "'I know the plans I have for you,' says the LORD.
'They are plans for good and not for disaster,
to give you a future and a hope'" (Jeremiah 29:11).

The prophet Jeremiah spoke those words to God's people as they were in captivity. But they are for us today too. God plans to use you. He has given you this time in your life with a lot of awesome adult supervision and coaching, tons of free time, no bills to pay or jobs to complete...to prepare you for your future.

What are two or three things you think God has made you good at?

_____

_____

_____

_____

_____

What do you *love* to do?

_____

_____

_____

_____

_____

_____

What could you do *now* to become excellent at the
things you are good at and love to do?

_____

_____

_____

_____

_____

_____

_____

SKG
Puzzle Craze

Find the following words in the word-search puzzle. Four of the words will not help you train for anything in life. Circle those four words in red.

TRAIN STRIVE LEARN COMPLAIN LAZY COACH
REST FOCUS WORK DISCIPLINE READ SWEAT
COUCH STUDY BOREDOM BELIEVE PRACTICE

```
I  P  N  K  G  H  V  L  P  T  Y  W  U  K  C
D  X  F  R  V  O  W  R  E  Z  B  F  W  O  Y
G  I  V  O  Q  Y  A  T  A  A  D  U  U  W  E
E  N  S  W  Y  C  P  L  L  L  R  C  V  X  W
Q  V  T  C  T  S  T  U  D  Y  H  N  S  C  Y
J  R  E  I  I  A  X  X  Z  V  N  R  R  U  Z
R  W  C  I  Y  P  E  T  X  O  O  F  C  H  K
A  E  P  Y  L  J  L  W  T  W  G  O  O  R  K
G  B  S  J  J  E  X  I  S  B  E  C  M  X  E
Y  M  G  T  T  B  B  D  N  J  V  U  P  C  Y
U  V  C  F  K  Y  Y  J  N  E  I  S  L  G  S
M  O  D  E  R  O  B  I  Z  G  R  E  A  D  Q
H  C  A  O  C  Q  A  C  O  J  T  Z  I  T  P
C  E  A  O  I  R  P  C  R  B  S  J  N  U  U
M  V  O  K  T  E  R  M  K  A  X  Y  S  C  R
```

For puzzle answers go to page 104.

Look Inside Yourself

I'm sure you found the four unhelpful words to be "lazy," "couch," "complain," and "boredom." Every day gives us a lot of hours to use up. Let's look at the four words of weakness we found in the puzzle and see if you are spending time there.

LAZY. Write down a story of the last time you remember being lazy. What could you have been doing instead?

_____

_____

_____

_____

_____

_____

THE COUCH. How much time each day do you spend sitting on your couch? _____ minutes

COMPLAINING. I probably complain (circle one: *one, two, five, more than ten*) times each day.

BOREDOM. What do you do when you feel bored?

_____

_____

_____

_____

A lot of us, when bored, turn to television, the computer, or food. Make a list of five things you could do instead of wasting time. We've given some hints to help you along, and we've simply provided the first one for you.

1. I could spend a little time with God reading the Bible and just talking to him.

2. Hint: What is found on a shelf in your house, has two covers, and has a lot to say?

I could _____.

3. Hint: What am I really good at?

I could practice _____.

4. Hint: Jesus came to serve, not to be served.

I could help _____

with _____.

5. Hint: Nothing is as good for the human body as fresh air.

I could go out and _____

or _____

or _____.

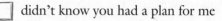

Wow, God.

I have to confess that I
(check all of the boxes that apply)…

- [ ] didn't know you had a plan for me
- [ ] wonder if you have really made me good at something
- [ ] can be super lazy
- [ ] spend a bunch of my free time complaining
- [ ] get bored really easily
- [ ] don't like working hard at anything
- [ ] waste a lot of time
- [ ] would like to become great at something

Reach Up to Talk to GOD

I'm excited about your promise that you have something planned for me. What I need to do now is use this time you've given me to prepare for your plans. Help me to use my time wisely. I know a lot of girls who are spending time chasing boys or dreaming about movie stars and singers. I…

- [ ] have been
- [ ] have not been

…one of those girls. Anyhow, from this day forward make me a girl who runs the race in a way that will help me win the prize! I'm ready to run. No shadowboxing for me!

Your champion,

_____

(Sign here)

Do You Know Jesus?

I remember the day I (Dannah) began my friendship with Jesus. I was four-and-a-half years old. I was at a neighborhood Bible club, where I had just heard that Jesus loved me and had died for me on the cross.

♡ John 3:16 says,

"God loved the world so much that he gave his one and only Son, so that everyone who believes in him will not perish but have eternal life."

The teacher told me that the reason Jesus had to die is because God is pure and holy and perfect and can't be near anything that is not. So, he can't be near sin. (Sinning is doing something bad or against God's plan.)

♡ Romans 3:23

"Everyone has sinned; we all fall short of God's glorious standard."

Any sin—even just one little one—separates us from God's perfection. I didn't want that. But I knew I had sinned. I wanted to live forever in heaven with Jesus, so I prayed a prayer that sounded a little like this:

Dear Jesus—
I know I have sinned. I know that this means I cannot live with you in heaven forever. I also know that you died to take the punishment for my sins. Will you forgive me? Come into my heart and be the God of my life. From this day forward, I want to be your friend.
In Your Name,
Amen!

I still remember what things were like that day. I remember the crack in the sidewalk that I saw as I prayed with my eyes open. I remember the smell of the evergreen trees nearby. I treasure that memory, and I know it was the beginning of my friendship with Jesus.

If you have never prayed a prayer like that, you can do it right now. Go get your mom or a teacher if you want someone to pray with you. But don't delay. Jesus wants to be your Best Friend!

Extra Ideas for Bible Study

You can do part two, the Secret Keeper Girl Bible study, all alone if you want to. But we have some other ideas for you in case you'd like to be creative:

Mother-Daughter Bible study

Your mom will learn as much as you will. You see, it's not me teaching, it's God. His Spirit is fully capable of helping your mom to meditate in a way that teaches her as she leads you. To do this with your mom, just get two copies and dig in. You can do it once a week or you can do it every day for a week.

Small group or Sunday school

How fun would it be to discuss all the great things you learn each week? You can do that by grabbing a group of friends to do this with. Do it after school once a week or in Sunday school every Sunday. We like to keep things simple with Secret Keeper Girl Bible studies, so you really don't need any extra books. If you're the leader, just select one appropriate question from each of the three sections:

- Dig In to Study
- Look Inside Yourself
- Reach Up to Talk to God

Be sure to enjoy some fun snacks at the beginning and to end in prayer!

Answers to Puzzle Crazes!

Answer to puzzle in Meditation #2, Page 66:

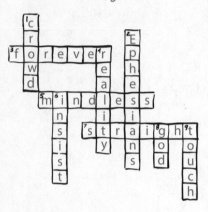

Answer to puzzle in Meditation #4, Page 82:

Answer to puzzle in Meditation #3, Page 75:

Answer to puzzle in Meditation #5, Page 88:

The wise person will listen to advice, making her wise and sure to succeed!

Answer to puzzle in Meditation #6, Page 98:

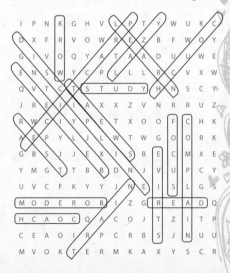

SECRET KEEPER GIRL® SERIES
A Girl's Guide to Best Friends and Mean Girls
with Suzy Weibel

If you're a girl, buckle up for some friendship drama. Some things about friendships are great, like BFFs—and some things are really hard, like dealing with mean girls!

In *A Girl's Guide to Best Friends and Mean Girls*, we help you rewrite the script to experience friendship with Jesus as your role model. Quizzes, puzzles, meditations, and biblical advice will help you get closer to him, your truly best friend. And as you do, you'll get better at being friends with everyone! You'll find answers to questions like these:

- Who should I choose for friends?
- What do I do about jealousy and hurts in my friendships? How about mean girls?
- How can I be Jesus' friend, and how do I introduce others to him?

A Girl's Guide to Best Friends and Mean Girls gives you everything you need to build better friendships.

And for you and your mom...

8 GREAT DATES

Talking with Your Daughter About Best Friends and Mean Girls

One of the best ways to guide your girl toward healthy friendships is to spend quality time with her yourself. The popular 8 Great Dates series from Secret Keeper Girl offers the most fun you'll ever have digging in to God's Word with your daughter. (Think: shopping sprees, slumber parties, ding-dong-ditching, and more!) Eight creative dates help you and your daughter tackle questions like...

- Why do I feel jealous of my BFF sometimes?
- How should I act when I get left out?
- Is it okay to be boy-crazy?

Creative ideas and godly guidance help you bond with your daughter and protect her as she navigates the crazy tween world of friendships using God's truth as her standard.

COMING TO A CITY NEAR YOU!

Our CRAZIEST show yet on practical modesty, fashion, & true beauty!

Dannah Gresh's
Secret Keeper GiRL
Crazy HaiR
→ TOUR!

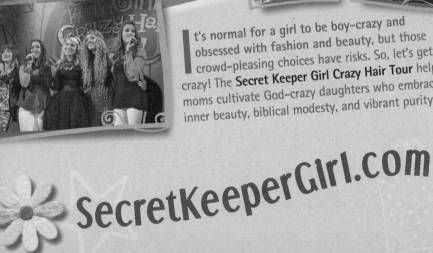

It's normal for a girl to be boy-crazy and obsessed with fashion and beauty, but those crowd-pleasing choices have risks. So, let's get crazy! The **Secret Keeper Girl Crazy Hair Tour** helps moms cultivate God-crazy daughters who embrace inner beauty, biblical modesty, and vibrant purity.

SecretKeeperGirl.com

What is a
Secret Keeper Girl?

Well, she's a lot of things. And she's NOT a lot of things. She's NOT a mean girl. She's a girl whose friendships are full of kindness. She's NOT boy crazy. (Moms, can we get an Amen?) She's a girl who knows she can share all of her heart-secrets with her mom at any time.

She's also a girl who embraces modesty. Why? Because she knows that she is a masterpiece created by God. She strives to keep the deepest secrets of her authentic beauty a secret! Maybe you are new to our movement, or maybe you are a long-time Secret Keeper Girl who has been to a live event. Maybe you have already read "Secret Keeper" and been on eight great dates with your Momma! Regardless, you, sweet girl, are a Secret Keeper Girl because you are a masterpiece created by God's hand.

Secret Keeper GIRL

SecretKeeperGirl.com

Like us on Facebook!
Follow us on Twitter!